THE MEDITERRANEAN COOKB(
BEGINNERS

Unlock The Flavors Of 2023 With The Ultimate Fresh, Wholesome Recipes And Embrace A No-Stress 8-Week Meal Plan

DANIEL OLMSTEAD

INTRODUCTION

Discover the vibrant flavors, aromatic herbs and sun-kissed ingredients that have long characterized Mediterranean cuisine. In "The Mediterranean Cookbook for Beginners", you will gain an introduction to its complex tapestry of flavors and time-honored traditions - while journeying across Greece, Italy, and Spain and beyond as you discover their roots of Mediterranean food! This cookbook promises an experience like no other as you discover these vibrant delights from their sun-drenched regions!

This cookbook serves as an excellent start line to find out Mediterranean delicacies. Whether you are a skilled chef or just beginning your culinary adventures, this book offers all of the information and competencies you need to craft flavorful yet nutritious dishes inspired by the usage of Mediterranean weight loss plan.

This book serves two capabilities: to introduce you to the Mediterranean diet and its health benefits; and provide realistic hints and steering on incorporating Mediterranean cooking into your life-style. What precisely is this weight-reduction plan, and why has it garnered such big interest amongst health fanatics and foodies alike? The Mediterranean diet is more than just another passing trend or restrictive regimen; it is an approach to life that recognizes and celebrates the abundance of fresh, whole food found throughout its region, taking its cue from those living on Mediterranean shores that have long enjoyed incredible longevity with reduced chronic disease risk. The Mediterranean diet has been related to improved brain health, including advanced cognitive performance and a lower chance of neurodegenerative problems like Alzheimer's and Parkinson's. The diet supplies critical vitamins, antioxidants, and wholesome fat that aid helps the mind through its emphasis on fruits, veggies, whole grains, legumes, seafood, and olive oil.

The Mediterranean diet has also been proven to lessen the danger of growing type 2 diabetes and aid in the control of the ailment in people who have already gotten it. Improved glycemic control and insulin sensitivity are effects of the Mediterranean diet's recognition on whole grains, fruits, vegetables, legumes, and olive oil whilst limiting consumption of processed foods and added sugars. A reduction in inflammation is beneficial because it lowers the threat of developing cardiovascular disorder, diabetes, and numerous malignancies. The Mediterranean diet is useful to health due to the fact it is high in anti-inflammatory meals such fruits, veggies, whole grains, fish, and olive oil.

Eating a Mediterranean-style dish has furthermore been connected to a reduced hazard of different cancers like breast, colorectal and prostate cancers. The food regimen's moderate consumption of fish and chicken, similarly to its high consumption of plant-based whole meals, antioxidants, and fiber, has a preventive impact in opposition to most cancers development. The Mediterranean diet is known for its useful results on digestive fitness due to its concentration on fiber-wealthy meals such fruits, greens, legumes, and whole grains. Consistent bowel actions, a healthy gut microbiota, and a reduced hazard of digestive troubles like constipation and diverticulitis are all advantages of eating a diet excessive in fiber.

Following a weight-reduction plan just like that of the Mediterranean has been related to higher health and a longer existence span. Incorporating nutrient-dense diets, appropriate fat, mild alcohol use (mostly crimson wine), and everyday exercise will enhance fitness and extend life.

Moreover, a lower risk of stroke has been associated with eating a Mediterranean eating regimen. Reduced risk of cardiovascular disorder and stroke may be at the least partly due to the food regimen's recommendation of a plant-based diet, the intake of healthy fat, and the moderation of alcoholic drinks.

At the core of Mediterranean nutrition lays fruits and vegetables, legumes, whole grains, nuts, and seeds—ingredients rich with natural flavors and essential nutrients. Olive oil stands out as an integral component of Mediterranean cuisine for both its taste and health benefits; seafood and lean proteins like poultry or beans are preferred to red and processed meats while herbs and spices add depth without adding excessive sodium or unhealthy seasonings to dishes.

Incorporating Mediterranean cooking into your lifestyle is both exciting and approachable, as this book will show you all of the essential techniques, kitchen tools, pantry essentials and pantry staples needed for culinary exploration. With our advice and suggestions you'll learn to craft balanced and flavorful meals that are not only delicious but nutritious as well. With Mediterranean ingredients spanning from light salads to satisfying stews you will learn to harness their unique flavors in dishes that range from light salads to filling stews - giving your palate something different every time!

Modern life can be hectic and demanding. That's why we provide practical tips for meal planning, time-saving strategies and adapting Mediterranean recipes to fit into busy schedules and preferences. No matter if you are a vegetarian, pescatarian or have special dietary requirements; we believe the Mediterranean diet can still deliver its extraordinary health benefits while meeting any specific dietary preferences or needs.

Are you ready for an epicurean journey that will transport your taste buds to sunny shores and embrace a way of eating that celebrates both pleasure and wellbeing? "The Mediterranean Cookbook for Beginners" will serve as your trusted partner on this voyage of discovery - indulge your senses with delicious flavors while adopting healthier lifestyle practices while unlocking its secrets with each delectable dish that passes by!

CHAPTER ONE: THE MEDITERRANEAN DIET BASICS

Understanding the Principles and Components of the Mediterranean Diet

The Mediterranean Diet has long been recognized for being among the healthiest and sustainable diet plans available today, drawing its inspiration from countries surrounding the Mediterranean Sea (such as Greece, Italy, Spain, Morocco, etc). Not only is its cuisine delicious and healthful - understanding its principles and components allows us to incorporate its practices into our daily lives and incorporate this diet as part of life-long health habits.

At its heart, Mediterranean diet emphasizes whole, unprocessed plant foods for good health; specifically fruits and vegetables which provide essential vitamins, minerals and fiber - from plump tomatoes and juicy cucumbers to colorful peppers and leafy greens! Mediterranean regions boast an abundance of nutrient-packed produce!

Beyond simply selecting and eating mindfully, Mediterranean dieting encompasses an approach of mindful eating that encourages individuals to savor every bite, recognize flavors and textures within meals and listen for hunger/satisfaction cues. Mindful eating fosters healthier relationships between food and its consumers by curbing overeating while creating greater bonds through dining experiences.

Additionally, social relationships and communal dining are integral parts of Mediterranean culture and form the backbone of its cuisine. Sharing meals with loved ones not only adds pleasure and increases happiness; such dining opportunities reflect how the Mediterranean lifestyle values both nourishment and social connections.

By understanding the principles and components of the Mediterranean diet, it enables us to enjoy delectable yet healthful eating patterns. Through adding plant-based foods, healthy fats, whole grains, lean proteins as well as herbs and spices into meals we can adopt this Mediterranean approach in our eating patterns and satisfy both body and taste buds alike! Mediterranean Cuisine Mediterranean cuisine is widely revered for its vibrant flavors, varied ingredients and remarkable health benefits. Originating in culinary traditions throughout countries along the Mediterranean Sea basin, its roots reveal an intricate network of staples which comprise its core essence - and by exploring these ingredients further we can unlock their mysteries ourselves and start an enriching culinary adventure!

It is essential to know that dairy products are an integral component of Mediterranean cuisine, yet should only be enjoyed sparingly. Yogurt and cheese in particular are revered ingredients which add creamy textures with subtly tart notes to various dishes - Greek Yogurt makes an appearance in breakfast dishes such as oatmeal while Feta Halloumi Ricotta bring salty-rich tastes into salads, pastries and other savories alike.

Nuts and seeds also play an essential part in Mediterranean cuisine, providing both texture and nutrition in one handy package. Almonds, walnuts, pistachios and pine nuts can be found both sweet and savory dishes for their satisfying crunch, healthy fat content and numerous vitamins and minerals; sesame seed varieties add both nutritional benefits as well as texture enhancing flavors to salads, dippers or baked goods while sesame, flaxseed and sunflower seed varieties add both textural benefits while simultaneously contributing both texture and nutritional values that enhance flavor profiles as well.

One of the key principles of the Mediterranean Diet is choosing whole, unprocessed foods as close to their natural state as possible, rather than resorting to processed or packaged products. By doing this, consumers benefit from receiving all of the valuable vitamins, minerals, phytochemicals and antioxidative compounds present within these fresh whole ingredients for maximum health benefits and well-being benefits. The Mediterranean Diet emphasizes food variety and seasonality through encouraging individuals to explore a wide variety of fruits, vegetables, grains and legumes - from colorful produce like fruits to legumes - thus meeting essential vitamins, minerals and antioxidant intake requirements. Plus embracing seasonal food allows one to take full advantage of peak flavors and nutritional contents of each item for an enhanced dining experience!

The Mediterranean diet is thus deeply rooted in its culinary traditions of its region. This way of eating celebrates both cooking as an art and sharing meals together; traditional methods, like grilling, roasting and sautéing are commonly employed to maximize flavor while attenuating fat consumption and oil use. By adopting such cooking practices you can produce satisfying yet delectable dishes while cutting back on excess calories from oils and fats.

Adopting the Mediterranean diet not only contributes to individual wellness but is also good for our planet, by supporting local farms that source locally grown seasonal foods that reduce emissions by less transportation. Adopting this eating lifestyle also promotes sustainable fishing practices which helps sustain biodiversity while supporting small scale agriculture with minimal ecological impact, thus contributing to more environmentally responsible ways of eating and contributing toward greater sustainability of ecosystems. By adopting it you're contributing towards more responsible ways of eating!

Exploring the key ingredients and staples of Mediterranean Cuisine

- Whole grains such as bulgur, quinoa and farro play an integral part in a Mediterranean diet by maintaining their original levels of natural fibers, vitamins, and minerals to provide more nutrition than refined versions. Perfect as the basis of comforting pilaf, comforting porridge or crusty loaf of bread - whole grains provide lasting energy that balance your diet in every sense!
- Legumes such as chickpeas, lentils and beans are essential parts of Mediterranean cuisine, serving not only as an excellent plant-based protein source but also being packed full of dietary fiber, iron and various key vitamins and minerals that provide heartiness texture and nutritional advantages - thus cementing their place among culinary records!
- Healthy fats found in olive oil, nuts and seeds play an integral part of a Mediterranean-style diet.
- Olive oil stands out for being packed full of monounsaturates and antioxidants, providing numerous health advantages; whether used on salads or as part of cooking methods; olive oil adds unique flavors while supporting cardiovascular wellbeing.
- Seafood, such as salmon, mackerel and sardines is an integral component of a Mediterranean diet. Packed full of omega-3 fatty acids associated with reduced heart disease risks and better brain performance; regular consumption provides lean proteins as well as essential vitamins needed to live an enduringly wholesome lifestyle diet.
- The Mediterranean diet promotes moderation in one's intake of dairy products like yogurt and cheese as sources of calcium, protein and probiotics that support bone health and gut microbiota. To stay on course with balance within ones diet it's crucial to select quality items while practicing portion control; something encouraged by The Mediterranean Diet.
- Red meat should not be completely excluded from a Mediterranean diet; rather, its consumption should be limited and prioritized towards leaner sources of lean protein such as poultry eggs and legumes as sources. Reducing red meat consumption aligns with principles of sustainable and healthful eating practices.
- The Mediterranean diet places great importance on flavor through herbs and spices such as basil, oregano, rosemary and thyme - to add depth and complexity in Mediterranean recipes – cumin coriander, cinnamon paprika spices are used liberally too for an authentic Mediterranean culinary experience! All without excess sodium intake!

Exploring the aforementioned key ingredients and staples of Mediterranean cuisine is an exciting journey into its delicious world of tantalizing flavors and nutritious fare, opening a gateway into delicious meals that promote overall well-being and promote overall wellness. Together we should embark upon this culinary voyage - its abundance of tasty flavors and nutritious qualities promise great rewards at every turn!

Benefits of Adopting a Mediterranean Lifestyle

Adopting the Mediterranean diet and lifestyle has garnered much praise due to its many health benefits, positive impacts on well-being and holistic approach that includes nutrition, physical activity, social networks and maintaining an overall balanced approach towards life. By adopting such ways of living individuals may experience numerous advantages which promote longevity, vitality and well-being.

One of the greatest advantages of adopting a Mediterranean-inspired lifestyle is improving cardiovascular wellness. Studies demonstrate how this diet, consisting of fruits, vegetables, whole grains, healthy fats and lean proteins such as olive oil's monounsaturates; omega-3 fatty acids found in fish; antioxidants present in plant foods all work to keep cholesterol at manageable levels while simultaneously decreasing inflammation for improved cardiovascular wellbeing.

Another key advantage of living the Mediterranean lifestyle lies in its positive effect on brain health. A diet rich in antioxidant-rich fruits, vegetables, olive oil and omega-3 fatty acids from fish helps safeguard cognitive function against age-related decline and neurodegenerative conditions like Alzheimer's. Furthermore, living this way promotes overall mental well-being via mindful eating practices, social ties and taking an overall balanced approach to life.

Weight management may be an ongoing warfare for plenty individuals. A Mediterranean-stimulated lifestyle offers one sustainable solution. Eating entire, unprocessed meals moderately with portion management and conscious ingesting helps to control appetites and restrict overeating; growing fiber-rich culmination, veggies and whole grains in food to promote feeling of fullness/delight for reduced energy intake; walking is some other effective method that simultaneously aids weight management while imparting fitness blessings.

Also, a Mediterranean life-style has long been related with decreased dangers of persistent illnesses, consisting of type 2 diabetes and certain cancers. By emphasizing whole meals resources with lots of healthful fats and low glycemic index carbohydrates for controlling blood sugar and improving insulin sensitivity degrees (a critical thing in controlling type 2 diabetes chance) together with providing adequate resources of antioxidant-rich and anti inflammatory compounds. Mediterranean delicacies may additionally doubtlessly offer protection from such varieties of ailment.

Mediterranean living promotes more than physical wellbeing; it emphasizes social connections and an overall balanced mindset as well. An emphasis on communal dining, shared meals between family and friends, food as an experience, and food as part of life gives a sense of belonging, happiness, and overall well-being that contributes to healthier eating habits as well as strengthening bonds, decreasing stress levels and cultivating an optimistic perspective on life.

Mediterranean lifestyle practices promote sustainability and environmental friendliness through emphasizing whole plant-based foods found at farmers markets or seasonal produce that is locally grown or a seasonal produce; by decreasing processed and heavily packaged food consumption this lifestyle supports sustainable agriculture while simultaneously decreasing carbon footprints; providing an eco-conscious nutrition approach.

CHAPTER TWO: ESSENTIAL COOKING TECHNIQUES

Introduction to fundamental cooking techniques used in Mediterranean Cuisine

Mediterranean cuisine is widely known for its vibrant flavors, stunning color combinations and wide array of delicious dishes. At its heart lies an ancient culinary tradition: grilling and roasting are among many fundamental techniques used in Mediterranean cooking to bring out the best from regional ingredients and create those distinctive Mediterranean tastes; braising and sautéing are among other techniques employed that transform simple ingredients into culinary works of art!

- Mediterranean cuisine's hallmark technique of grilling has long been recognized for its signature smoky char and ability to bring out natural flavors - be they succulent meat slices marinated with spices and sauces or tender vegetables and seafood; grilling creates the delicious contrast between crisp exteriors and tender, succulent interiors, making outdoor markets and street food stands all across Mediterranean regions all the more convenient places for people to gather over delicious meals al fresco!
- Roasting is another essential aspect of Mediterranean cuisine. Roasting involves heating food to high temperatures using either an oven or open flame in order to intensify flavors by caramelizing natural sugars for more intense, tender, flavorful dishes. Roasted vegetables such as tomatoes, peppers and eggplant become delicious spreads or sauces while meat such as whole chickens or lamb is often marinated with fragrant herbs and spices for elegant centerpieces at Mediterranean feasts.
- Braising is an ancient slow cooking method which involves simmering food over low heat for extended periods. Braising works especially well when applied to tough cuts of meat or root vegetables as the gentle simmering breaks down their fibers to produce tender and flavorful meals. Braising dishes often incorporate aromatic vegetables, herbs and spices that add depth and complexity - from Moroccan tagines to Greek stifado braising are revered techniques which bring both depth and tenderness to Mediterranean fare.
- Sautéing (or shallow frying), is an efficient cooking technique used for quickly heating ingredients with small amounts of fat at high heat to develop both rich flavor and crisp textures quickly and efficiently. Sautéing works especially well when applied to vegetables like zucchini, mushrooms or spinach which are sautéed quickly in olive oil or butter before being enhanced by herbs and spices for Mediterranean-style meals that use this cooking style.
- Steaming is an efficient yet delicate cooking technique which uses steam to preserve natural flavors, colors, and nutrients of ingredients in their most original forms. Steam is frequently utilized by Mediterranean cuisine chefs when working with vegetables, seafood or grains - especially vegetables that feature juicy or tender results from this technique! Steamed dishes showcase fresh produce at its purest state!
- Marinating ingredients in an aromatic blend of herbs, spices, oils and acids to impart depth and complexity into dishes like souvlaki or vegetable grilling marinades is another integral element of Mediterranean cooking that ensures its delicious flavors permeate every bite.

Understanding these fundamental cooking techniques allows us to tap the true spirit of Mediterranean cooking. From grilling, roasting, braising, sautéing and steaming dishes we make; every technique adds unique flavors and textures which further depth our meals with Mediterranean flair! By mastering all these methods we can fully appreciate their diversity and richness while infusing meals with its magic while tantalizing palates with Mediterranean flavor!

Tips for Selecting and Preparing Fresh Ingredients

Mediterranean cuisine relies heavily on ingredients of exceptional quality and freshness in order to produce memorable dishes, from vibrant fruits and vegetables, succulent seafood and aromatic herbs - to ensure our meals contain natural goodness while exuding vibrant color! By following some simple rules we can guarantee our meals reflect this vibrant cuisine with ease!

- **Shopping at Local Farmers' Markets:** Farmers' markets offer fresh seasonal produce straight from local growers at peak ripeness for optimal flavor and nutritional benefits. It is important to shop from Local Farmers' Markets, as it aids in getting the freshest ingredients.
- To properly select fresh produce, it's essential that we utilize all five senses when making decisions regarding produce selection. Sight, touch, and smell can provide us with guidance towards quality produce; start by checking fruits and vegetables for firmness and vibrancy before searching out vibrant hues that indicate freshness; check for signs such as bruised edges or discolorations that indicate their shelf-life has expired.
- **Buy Seasonal Produce:** When selecting ingredients to use in recipes, opt for seasonal produce as it tends to provide optimal flavors, textures, and nutritional profiles. Seasonal fruits and veggies tend to be both more affordable and sustainable options.
- **Consider Organic Produce:** Produce grown without synthetic pesticides and fertilizers is often healthier for both the environment and you - look out for products labeled "Certified Organic."
- **Search Locally Sourced Fish and Seafood:** When choosing fish and seafood, prioritize local options first. Freshness is of the utmost importance so select fish with clear eyes, shiny skin, mild scent and non-fishy textures such as slimy or smelly varieties.
- **Explore the Deli Section:** Mediterranean cuisine is famed for its abundance of cured meats, cheeses, olives and preserved ingredients that add authentic flavors and textures. When visiting your local deli or specialty store, search for authentic options and add them into your dishes.
- **Choose Extra Virgin Olive Oil:** Olive oil is an integral component of Mediterranean cooking; therefore it makes sense to select extra virgin olive oil for its superior taste and health benefits. When choosing brands or certifying seals such as International Olive Council's (IOC), make sure they offer exceptional taste as well.
- **Prioritize Fresh Herbs:** Fresh herbs like basil, parsley, oregano and mint are key elements in Mediterranean cuisine. Choose vibrantly-colored plants without signs of discoloration for optimal freshness - consider cultivating your own supply to ensure continuous availability!
- **Check for Whole Grains:** Mediterranean cuisine includes numerous whole grains such as bulgur, quinoa and farro that should be purchased whole and unprocessed without added preservatives or flavorings. When buying these grains ensure they contain nothing artificial such as preservatives.
- **Support Local and Sustainable Practices:** Consider supporting farmers, fishermen and food producers who prioritize sustainable and ethical practices as this not only gives you access to fresher ingredients but also contributes to local economies while decreasing your environmental footprint.
- Texture-wise, fruits and vegetables differ considerably when it comes to their firmness or yielding nature; certain fruits such as tomatoes should feel firm while yielding slightly when pinched; in comparison, leafy greens such as spinach or lettuce must maintain crisp textures free from signs of wilting or sliminess.
- Finding fresh ingredients requires using your nose. Sniffing their aroma can provide invaluable clues as to whether ingredients have reached peak freshness levels; herbs such as basil, mint and rosemary should have strong yet aromatic odors that indicate freshness while citrus melons such as nectarines may give off sweet aromas signaling their peak freshness levels. Trusting your nose allows for accurate assessment.

Remember, selecting fresh ingredients is just step one in developing delicious Mediterranean dishes. Proper storage, handling, and cooking techniques also play an important position in maintaining the integrity and taste of the ingredients.

Once you've selected and purchased fresh Mediterranean ingredients, proper preparation is critical in maximizing their flavors and nutrients. Here are a few recommendations to ensure they get used efficiently:

- Before using fruits, vegetables or herbs it's imperative that they are washed to eliminate dirt, pesticides or bacterial contamination. Use cool running water while gently rubbing their surface if required to ensure maximum safety and cleanliness for your ingredients! This step ensures optimal safety and quality results!

- **Careful Handling of Delicate Ingredients:** Handling delicate ingredients such as herbs and berries requires special consideration in order to preserve their integrity and visual appeal. A light touch approach should be employed so as to maintain these items for as long as possible.

- **Chopping With Precision:** For accurate cutting of fruits, vegetables and herbs it is imperative that sharp knives with proper techniques for clean cuts are used - this not only enhances their visual presentation, but also facilitate even cooking and ensure optimal texture is created during processing. Investing in an excellent, sharp knife will allow for precise cuts that preserve and showcase fresh ingredients while improving presentation. A quality blade ensures clean cuts for precise preparations of ingredients while upholding integrity and aesthetic. By following these practices it will create presentable pieces as well as ensure appropriate texture is created while creating optimal processing results.

- **Store Appropriately:** Proper storage conditions can ensure freshness. Some fruits and vegetables prefer being kept cold while others can benefit from being kept at room temperature; knowing which method best works will extend its shelf life while protecting its flavors and prolong shelf life.

- **Learn the Basic Knife Skills:** Brush up on basic knife skills to ensure efficient and safe food preparation. Techniques such as dicing, chopping, mincing and julienning will enable you to achieve consistent pieces of ingredients - which are essential for even cooking!

- **Remove Blemishes:** Inspect and discard produce that contains any visible blemishes or damaged portions prior to cooking in order to maintain quality ingredients that won't introduce unwanted flavors or textures into final dishes. This step helps preserve overall quality ingredients.

- **Cut to Fit the Recipe Needs:** Before beginning any dish you are creating, carefully consider its specific requirements before cutting and slicing ingredients accordingly. Some dishes require thin slices while others call for larger chunks; by adapting their size and shape accordingly you ensure even cooking and an evenly dispersed flavor profile.

- **Blanching and Shock Greens:** When cooking recipes that feature greens like spinach or Swiss chard, blanching and shocking them in an ice bath will help preserve their vibrant color, texture, and nutritional value. This process involves briefly boiling them then immediately placing them into an ice bath to stop their cooking process.

- **Marinate to Infuse Flavors:** Marinating ingredients can add depth and complexity to Mediterranean dishes. Create your marinade using olive oil, fresh herbs, citrus juices and spices and let the food marinade for several hours or overnight before grilling, roasting or adding salad ingredients.

- **Preserve Citrus Zest:** Lemon or orange zest adds vibrant and refreshing flavor to a variety of Mediterranean dishes, particularly citrus juice drinks. Before using your citrus for juice extraction, peel its outer colored layer using either a zester or microplane and store the leftover zest in an airtight container in either your freezer or refrigerator for later use.

- **Toast Nuts and Seeds:** Nuts and seeds are an integral component of Mediterranean cuisine, and toasting can enhance their natural flavors and textures. Heat a dry skillet over medium heat before adding your nuts or seeds; make sure not to burn them as this could quickly lead to bitter flavors developing!

- **Maintain Herb Freshness:** Fresh herbs play a pivotal role in Mediterranean cooking. To keep them at their freshest, trim off their stem ends and arrange them in a glass of water like flowers in a bouquet, covering loosely with plastic bags before placing in the fridge - regularly updating this water as needed to increase freshness.
- **Utilize Seasonal Produce:** Mediterranean cuisine places immense value on seasonal produce due to its superior flavors and nutritional benefits; so embrace its bounty every season by selecting and including ingredients at their peak of taste and nutrients - not only will you reap its satisfying flavorful experience but by supporting local farmers you also reduce ecological impact!
- **Do Not Overcook:** Mediterranean cooking relies heavily on its hallmark ability of emphasizing on natural flavors and textures of fresh ingredients without overcooking, to preserve vibrant hues, textures and nutrients while creating appealing dishes! Aim for balance between raw and cooked elements when creating appealing plates!

Kitchen Equipments and Tools for Mediterranean Cooking

Before diving in and exploring Mediterranean cuisine, it's essential that your kitchen be fully-equipped. From basic tools such as wooden utensils to cutting edge gadgets, having all of the essential kitchen tools will streamline your experience in the kitchen and allow you to fully immerse yourself into its techniques and flavors. Here we explore essential tools used when creating dishes with Mediterranean style.

- **Chef's Knife:** Every kitchen requires an effective chef's knife. Mediterranean cooking relies heavily on it as part of its arsenal. From cutting vegetables and herbs, to slicing meats and seafood, an effective chef's knife enables accurate cutting that produces consistent culinary masterpieces.
- **Cutting Board:** When it comes to safe food prep, an efficient cutting board is indispensable. Wood or plastic models tend to be easier for keeping clean while providing stable surfaces for cutting ingredients such as vegetables.
- **Mortar and Pestle:** Mortar and pestle are traditional tools found in Mediterranean cuisine designed to pulverize herbs, spices, and other ingredients into powder form in order to release essential oils that add depth and complexity to dishes. By manually grinding ingredients you are also unlocking essential oils while flavoring each recipe further with their specific essential oils and flavors.
- **Citrus Juicer:** With Mediterranean fruits being such an abundant source of citrus juice, having access to one is invaluable in extracting fresh and vibrant citrus juice for use in salad dressing, marinating meat or flavoring sauces without seeds or pulp becoming an obstacle! A citrus juicer makes extraction straightforward!
- **Grill or Grill Pan:** When it comes to Mediterranean cooking techniques, grilling is at the core. A grill or grill pan offers all of the tools required for creating that iconic charred flavor and look on meats, vegetables and seafood alike - be it traditional outdoor grilling methods or stovetop pan cooking methods, having one at your disposal will allow you to craft amazing Mediterranean meals!
- Cast iron skillets are versatile pieces of cookware perfect for Mediterranean cuisine, offering even heat distribution while maintaining heat for multiple cooking techniques like sautéing, searing and frying. Cast iron skillets make delicious paella, frittatas or homemade bread dishes!
- **Ovenproof Baking Dish:** Mediterranean cuisine boasts an incredible diversity of baked dishes, from roast vegetables and casseroles to creamy gratins. An ovenproof baking dish allows you to effortlessly craft these delicacies without incurring added stress during preparation or serving time. When searching for such an investment piece, look for sturdy models featuring heat resistance as well as sizes to meet all of your baking

requirements.

- **Immersion Blender or Hand Blender**: An immersion blender (hand blender) is an efficient tool designed to quickly blend soups, sauces and dressings directly in their pot or bowl without needing to transfer hot liquids separately into another container for processing - offering smooth textures almost immediately! An immersion blender enables smooth results in mere moments!
- **Salad Spinner:** Crisp salads are an integral element of Mediterranean cuisine. A salad spinner provides efficient cleaning and drying of leafy greens to maintain crispiness when making each salad for guests, in addition to providing assistance when cleaning delicate ingredients like herbs.
- **Stainless Steel Mixing Bowls:** Every kitchen should possess at least a set of durable yet easy to maintain stainless steel mixing bowls in various sizes for mixing, tossing and marinating ingredients as well as for storage prepped ingredients in the fridge. Not only are stainless steel bowls durable yet easy to keep cleanly; they're stainless and odor proof!

By stocking up with these essential tools and equipment, your kitchen will be well equipped for Mediterranean culinary art. Not only can these tools and items increase efficiency during your cooking process; they'll allow you to discover all of the flavors and techniques associated with Mediterranean cuisine! Get equipped now so you can embark on this culinary adventure that celebrates this vibrant world of Mediterranean flavors!

CHAPTER THREE: BREAKFAST AND BRUNCH DELIGHTS

Fresh and Nutritious Breakfast Recipes to start your day

Breakfast is often considered the cornerstone of daily nutrition, and Mediterranean cuisine recognizes this by offering tantalizing breakfast/brunch offerings packed with energy-giving fruits, veggies, grains and dairy products - starting each morning off right and providing energy boost. Let us discover some delectable Mediterranean options sure to set off an energetic morning!

- **Mediterranean Omelet**

Here's a recipe for Mediterranean Omelet:

Ingredients:

- 1 tablespoon of olive oil
- 3 big eggs
- ¼ cup of chopped red onion
- ¼ cup of diced bell peppers
- ¼ cup of chopped sun-dried tomatoes
- ¼ cup of sliced black olives
- ¼ cup of crumbled feta cheese
- Pepper
- Salt
- Fresh basil or parsley leaves (optional)

Instructions:

- Crack the big eggs and put them into a mixing bowl.
- Beat the eggs lightly with a whisk or alternatively a fork.
- Add reasonable amount of salt and pepper to the mixture.
- Heat the olive oil in an omelet pan above medium heat.
- Put the bell peppers and red onion to the pan and sauté them for about 3 minutes until they become soft.
- Add black olive slices and diced tomato to the pan for another 1-2 minutes of cooking before including olives and diced tomato as desired.
- Store vegetables in an airtight bowl to maintain freshness.
- Add one additional tablespoon of oil and warm the pan over a low-medium temperature setting.
- Pour the beaten eggs into a pan and tilt it slightly so they spread out evenly.
- Before stirring or altering their shape, allow at least a minute for their edges to begin hardening and begin firming up.
- Add cooked greens on top of your eggs before topping with crumbled feta.
- Fold one side of your omelet over into a half moon shape to achieve even results, pressing lightly with a spatula for best results.
- Continue cooking the eggs until they have set completely and the cheese has completely melted, usually taking around one more minute.
- Place the omelet onto a plate and decorate as desired; for instance, chopped parsley or basil could add extra flair!

Serve this tasty and nutritious treat alongside whole-grain toast or mixed green salad for the ideal breakfast meal!

- **Greek Yoghurt Parfait:** Experience an irresistibly delectable Greek Yogurt Parfait! Enjoy its delightful combination of creamy Greek Yogurt with layers of fresh fruits and crunchy toppings that creates an irresistibly delectable treat! Here's a recipe for Greek Yoghurt Parfait:

Ingredients:

- 1 cup of Greek yogurt
- 1 cup of mixed berries (for instance, strawberries, blueberries)
- 1 cup of granola
- Honey or maple syrup (optional)
- Diced nuts or seeds (optional)

Instructions:

- For optimal results, choose an opaque glass or bowl to layer your parfait in.
- Start layering by spreading one tablespoon of Greek yogurt evenly along the base of your glass or bowl, before spreading another spoonful evenly along its length to form an even surface layer.
- Sprinkle granola over yogurt as desired - either your go-to favorite granola from store options, or make your own to personalize!
- Top the granola with an assortment of mixed fruits to give it depth in terms of colors and flavors. Try using an individual type or multiple types for variety in terms of both hue and taste.
- Repeat these layers until the glass is full; top off the last one with more yogurt, berries, granola and fruit for an appealing treat! Finish by topping your final layer off with more berries for the finishing touch!
- As for sweeter parfaits, honey or maple syrup drizzle can add additional sweetness and you can customize to meet your own personal preferences.
- Add extra nutrition and crunch with almonds or walnuts sprinkled onto the top layer.
- Serve immediately or allow to chill briefly to allow all the flavors to combine before enjoying!

Now you can enjoy Greek Yogurt parfait as a healthy and refreshing breakfast, snack or dessert option! Simply customize the parfait by incorporating nuts, fruits or cinnamon to suit your personal preferences and create your very own personalized parfait experience!

- **Shakshuka:** This popular North African and Middle Eastern breakfast option has become a classic Mediterranean fare, featuring vibrant tomato-bell pepper sauce simmered with spices like cumin, paprika, and chili flakes. Here's a recipe for Shakshuka:

Ingredients:

- 2 tablespoons of olive oil
- 1 thinly sliced onion
- 1 thinly sliced red bell pepper
- 2 cloves of garlic, minced
- 1 teaspoon of ground cumin
- 1 teaspoon of ground paprika
- 1/2 teaspoon of ground cayenne pepper (adjust to your spice preference)
- 1 can (400g) of crushed tomatoes
- Salt
- Pepper
- 4-6 large eggs
- Fresh parsley or cilantro, chopped (for garnish)
- Crusty bread or pita, for serving

Instructions:

- Tumble olive oil in a big frying pan over medium-low heat till bubbling for approximately 2-3 minutes.

- Add bell pepper and onion slices to the warm pan, sautéing for five minutes, till greens begin to soften.
- Add floor cumin, cayenne pepper, minced garlic and floor paprika and cook dinner for one more minute to allow those spices to release their full array of flavors.
- Add crushed tomatoes, season with pepper and salt, and carefully blend all of the substances.
- Reduce the heat, and simmer the sauce for 10-15 minutes before switching it back on to medium.
- Create small indentations in the sauce using a wooden spoon and drop one egg into each one of these wells.
- Poach the eggs by covering your skillet or pan and poaching in their sauce until just before they have set - yet remain runny in texture - according to your taste preferences and cooking time requirements. Adjust accordingly!
- Remove your skillet from the heat. Decorate it with chopped parsley, cilantro or both to further enhance its look.
- Serve this Shakshuka dish with pita bread or crusty bread on the side to easily scoop up sauce and eggs from its surface.

Shakshuka can be prepared in various ways. Add ingredients like feta cheese or spinach for an irresistibly delicious and comforting dish ideal for brunch, breakfast, lunchtime meals and quick bites on-the-go!

- **Mediterranean fruit salad**

Here's a recipe for Mediterranean fruit salad:
Ingredients:

- 2 cups of mixed fresh fruits (for instance watermelon, grapes, strawberries, and pineapple)
- Cut the mixed fruits into bite-sized pieces
- 1 tablespoon of fresh lemon juice
- 1 tablespoon of fresh orange juice
- 1 tablespoon of honey or maple syrup (optional)
- Diced Fresh mint leaves

Instructions:

- Slice fruits into bite-size chunks after washing and prepping them, choosing varieties you enjoy or are in season for this snack.
- Mix all the fruits together in a large bowl.
- Add orange and lemon juices together in a small dish and whisk. You may add maple syrup or honey for additional sweetening if desired; mix until everything has combined thoroughly.
- Pour the citrus mixture over the fruit in your bowl and toss gently so as to fully cover them in this fruit dressing.
- Allow the fruit to take in all of the dressings and flavors by leaving it sit in the refrigerator for 15-30 minutes before refrigerating it.
- Before serving a fruit salad, garnish it with freshly chopped mint leaves to bring an aromatic freshness and boost Mediterranean flavors.

Refrigerate Mediterranean Fruit Salad to serve it chilled as either an indulgent and healthy dessert or side for your grilled meats. Tastefully customize your fruit salad by including other seasonal and tasty fruits such as kiwi or mango, then top it off with citrus dressing for an irresistibly delicious Mediterranean experience!

- **Avocado Toast:** Take avocado toast beyond its classic form by infusing Mediterranean flavors and ingredients into it. Here's a recipe for Avocado Toast:

Ingredients:

- 1 ripe avocado
- 1 tablespoon of lemon juice
- 2 slices of bread (for instance whole wheat)
- Salt
- Pepper
- Red pepper flakes or cherry tomatoes (optional toppings)

Instructions:

- The Avocado should be cut lengthwise into halves.

- Scoop out and collect all of its flesh.
- Use a fork to mash avocado to your preferred texture - smooth or chunky is up to you.
- Add lemon juice to the avocado mixture for maximum protection and refreshing tang. Lemon will prevent it from turning brown over time while lending an irresistibly fresh edge.
- Add salt and pepper according to your tastes for optimal seasoning of the mixture. Make it your own.
- Toast bread slices until they turn golden brown using either a toaster-oven, regular oven, or both methods of toasting.
- Spread mashed avocado evenly on each piece of toast bread.
- Make this dish uniquely your own by being creative! For an extra zing, sprinkle red pepper flakes over your pasta; for some freshness add cherry tomato slices; crumble some feta for some tartiness or garnish the dish with micro greens and radishes for texture and extra taste! Feel free to experiment and adjust toppings according to personal taste!
- Serve avocado toast as soon as possible while the bread remains hot and crunchy.

Avocado toast can be tailored to suit individual preferences by including other elements, such as poached egg, bacon, smoked salmon or tuna - making this dish both healthy and delectable! Perfect for brunch, breakfast or an early snack option!

- **Overnight Chia Pudding:** For an easy and nutritious breakfast option, create an overnight chia pudding! Here's a recipe for Overnight Chia Pudding:

Ingredients:

- 1/4 cup of chia seeds
- 1 cup milk of your choice (for instance almond milk or dairy milk)
- 1 tablespoon sweetener of your choice (for instance honey or maple syrup)
- 1/2 teaspoon of vanilla extract (optional)
- Fresh fruits, nuts or seeds, (Optional toppings)

Instructions:

- In a bowl/jar, combine chia seed, sweetener and vanilla extract. Make sure all of the chia seeds are evenly dispersed across the mixture by stirring it thoroughly.
- After 5 minutes, give the mixture another stir so as to prevent clumping.
- Refrigerate bowl/jar and place overnight or for at least 4-6 hours; the chia seed will absorb liquid during this time and create a pudding-like texture.
- Stir your chia puding thoroughly either early in the morning, or just prior to serving to ensure a smooth consistency and no lumps.
- Add desired toppings if desired - such as fresh fruits, nuts and seeds, granola or coconut flakes to improve its texture, taste and nutritional value.
- Chia pudding can be enjoyed hot or chilled; enjoy it alone or layer in an attractive presentation jar to achieve optimal visual aesthetic.

Explore different flavors or toppings when creating overnight chia pudding, from cocoa powder for chocolaty tastes, mashed fruit for sweetness or spices like cinnamon and cardamom for spiced spice up this deliciously nutritious and convenient breakfast choice! Make it ahead and you will have breakfast waiting when you wake up the following morning.

Start each morning off right by including healthy breakfast recipes into your routine - not only will they taste delectably delicious, but you will be providing your body with essential vitamins and nutrients needed to set off each day in an upbeat way! Mediterranean-inspired dishes celebrate simplicity while adding vitality and flavor. So get up early to experience one of these delectable breakfast or brunch delights and set the stage for an energetic and fulfilling day ahead.

Delicious and Satisfying Brunch for Weekends and Special Occasions

Brunch is an enjoyable event which blends breakfast and lunch into one delicious dining experience, providing us with delicious yet filling meals at leisurely pace. Mediterranean cooking adds vivid flavors and rich culinary traditions; make this weekend gathering or special celebration even more enjoyable by including Mediterranean themed brunch recipes in your menu plan.

- **Mediterranean Bruschetta**

Here's a recipe for Mediterranean Brushetta:

Ingredients:

- 4-6 slices of baguette or Italian bread
- 1/4 cup of finely chopped red onion
- 2-3 diced ripe tomatoes
- 2 minced cloves of garlic
- 1 tablespoon of extra-virgin olive oil
- 1/4 cup of diced Kalamata olives
- 2 tablespoons of diced fresh basil leaves
- 2 tablespoons of diced fresh parsley
- 1 tablespoon balsamic vinegar (optional)
- Salt
- Pepper

Instructions:

- By preheating to 375degF, preheat your oven.
- Place slices of bread onto a baking tray and drizzle them with olive oil earlier than toasting in an preheated oven for eight-10 minutes, till their surface turns golden-brown and crisp - watch cautiously to avoid burning!
- Mix collectively chopped tomatoes, minced onion, Kalamata Olives, parsley basil and garlic in a big mixing bowl for max effect.
- Pour the extra virgin olive oil over the tomato and mix till all components are lightly covered with it. You could also strive including balsamic for an added tang.
- Adjust the seasoning according to your own taste by using salt and pepper according to what appeals most. You may adjust it until it meets your standards for perfect seasoning!
- After taking them out of the oven, allow time for them to cool for at least 5-10 minutes before placing back inside again.
- Be sure to divide the Mediterranean tomato mixture evenly amongst each of your bread slices.
- Serve Mediterranean bruschetta quickly to allow its flavors to come together, for an enticing and delectable appetizer which pairs beautifully with other Mediterranean fare.
- Add other Mediterranean ingredients such as feta crumbles, roasted peppers or pesto for a personalized brunch! Enjoy all its vibrant Mediterranean flavors on any special occasion with this versatile meal!

- **Spanakopita:** As a classic Greek dish, spanakopita makes for the ideal brunch food!

Here's the recipe:

Ingredients:

- 1 pound (450g) of trimmed fresh spinach
- 1/2 pound (225g) of crumbled feta cheese
- 1/2 cup of diced fresh dill
- 1/4 cup chopped fresh parsley
- 4 finely chopped green onions
- 2 tablespoons olive oil
- 3 eggs, lightly beaten
- Salt
- Pepper
- 12 sheets of phyllo pastry
- 1/2 cup melted butter or olive oil for brushing

Instructions:

- Preheat the oven to 375 degF before starting this recipe, lightly oil or spray the baking dish you will be using and set it aside.
- Start by bringing salted water to a rolling boil in a large pot, before adding spinach leaves for blanching for two minutes in boiling water before draining, cooling, squeezing out any extra moisture, cutting finely into smaller pieces for serving and serving immediately.
- Combine spinach, feta crumbles, dill, parsley and green onion in a large bowl with olive oil and an egg for flavor enhancement before seasoning to your preference with salt and pepper to suit. Gently fold all ingredients until evenly mixed.
- To prevent sheets from drying quickly, open them out and store them under damp kitchen towels.
- Place one phyllo sheet onto a clean surface. Brush lightly with either olive oil or melted butter before layering another sheet atop this one - repeat this step six times!
- Layer each sheet of phyllo with spinach-and-cheese mixture for even coverage.
- Glaze each layer of phyllo pastry with either melted butter or olive oil before stacking and baking it.
- Cut through the top layer of phyllo with a sharp knife into square or triangular pieces to form squared or triangular segments for scoring.
- Baking time will vary according to oven settings: 35-40 minutes at 325o F will deliver golden and crunchy results, depending on their own oven configurations.
- When you are done baking, remove from the oven and let it to cool for some minutes before refrigerating it.

- **Quiche:** An elegant and versatile dish, quiche can easily be customized for Mediterranean ingredients. Quiche is a delicious meal that has a savory custard filling baked in a pie crust. Here's a basic recipe and on how to prepare Quiche:

Ingredients:

- 1 pie crust (store-bought or homemade)
- 4 large eggs
- 1 cup of milk or heavy cream
- 1 cup grated cheese (for instance, Swiss or Cheddar)
- 1 cup cooked and chopped vegetables or meat (for instance, spinach, bacon)
- 1/2 teaspoon of salt
- 1/4 teaspoon of black pepper
- 1/4 teaspoon of nutmeg (optional)

Instructions:

- Preheat the oven to 375degF and follow any specific packaging directions if purchasing premade pie crust from your grocery store.
- Combine salt, pepper and nutmeg with eggs, cream or milk in a large mixing bowl and whisk to incorporate.
- Press your unbaked or prebaked pie crust firmly against the bottom and sides of a tart dish or pie dish for even distribution of heat during baking.
- Grated cheddar should be evenly spread on the base of your pie crust.
- Distribute evenly the chopped and cooked vegetables or meat on top of the cheese.
- Pour the egg mixture gradually over your fillings and cheese, taking care to cover everything evenly.
- Shake the pie dish gently so that all of the mixture settles evenly in its place.
- Bake the quiche for 30-35 minutes or until its top has turned golden-brown and its filling has set up completely.
- Let the quiche rest for several moments prior to cutting and serving.

Quiche can be enjoyed both warm and at room temperature; making it the ideal brunch, light dinner, or lunch option. Customize its filling to meet your preferences by including bell peppers or sautéed onions as desired - add fruit salad for a complete meal experience.

- **Lemon Ricotta Pancakes:** Lemon Ricotta Pancakes are fluffy and sourish pancakes made with ricotta cheese and fresh lemon zest. Here's a recipe and on how to prepare these delicious pancakes:

Ingredients:

- 1 cup of all-purpose flour
- 1 tablespoon of granulated sugar
- 1 teaspoon of baking powder
- 1/2 teaspoon of baking soda
- 1/4 teaspoon salt
- 3/4 cup of ricotta cheese
- 2 big eggs
- 1/2 cup milk
- Zest of 1 lemon
- 2 tablespoons of fresh lemon juice
- 1 teaspoon of vanilla extract
- Butter or oil for greasing the pan
- Maple syrup and fresh berries for serving (optional)

Instructions:

- Take out a big bowl and a whisk.
- Thoroughly mix the flour, sugar and baking soda/powder together.
- Blend the ricotta, eggs, lemon zest and juice, vanilla extract, milk, and lemon juice in a big mixing bowl.
- Mix together moist and dry ingredients till all has come collectively; don't overdo this step though as some lumps in your batter might also still continue to be; that is perfectly perfect!
- Before preheating food on your nonstick skillet or griddle on medium-low heat, grease its surface with oil or butter before pre-heating your meals in it.
- Apply the batter with the lower back cease of a spoon in an excellent circular pattern and bake for 2 to three mins, until bubbles seem on its surface and edges have hardened.
- Turnover and prepare dinner until they emerge as golden-brown and cooked very well; approximately some other one or two minutes need to do it.
- Cover each pancake with a kitchen towel before moving them onto a plate; this can preserve them warm whilst you finish using all ultimate batter for pancakes. Repeat this step as essential till all remaining batter has been used up.
- Serve heat Lemon Ricotta Pancakes with Maple Syrup, clean Berries and any additional preferred toppings if preferred.

Enjoy these pleasant pancakes warm and fresh to enjoy their complete blessings: creamy texture from the ricotta cheese combined with tart lemon zest creates an irresistibly delectable breakfast or brunch deal with!

- **Mediterranean Egg Bake:**

Mediterranean Egg Bake is a delicious and healthy brunch meal that combines eggs with Mediterranean ingredients like vegetables, herbs, and feta cheese. Here's a recipe on how to prepare Mediterranean Egg Bake:

Ingredients:

- 1 tablespoon olive oil
- 1 diced small onion
- 1 chopped bell pepper (any color you prefer)
- 2 minced cloves garlic
- 1 cup of cherry tomatoes, halved
- 1 cup of spinach leaves
- 1 teaspoon of dried oregano
- 1/2 teaspoon of dried thyme
- Salt
- Pepper
- 6 big eggs
- 1/4 cup of milk
- 1/2 cup of crumbled feta cheese
- Fresh basil or parsley leaves for garnish (optional)

Instructions:

- Preheat the oven to 375degF after which grease your baking dish the use of either cooking spray or olive oil.
- On medium warmth, warm up the olive oil earlier than adding diced bell peppers and onion for five mins or until soft.
- Continue to cook dinner the garlic until aromatic - about one more minute must do the trick!
- Add spinach leaves, oregano and dried thyme to the skillet along with salt and pepper; combine all the ingredients while continuing to stir over a low flame until tomatoes have softened somewhat and spinach has begun wilting - about 2-3 more minutes more if necessary.
- Spread evenly onto a baking dish.
- Combine milk and eggs together in a separate mixing bowl; season as desired with salt and pepper for desired flavors.
- Pour the egg mixture carefully over the vegetables cooked in your baking dish.
- Crumble some crumbled feta into the egg mixture for added flair.
- Bake the baking dish for 20-25 minutes or until the egg has set and has taken on a golden hue on its pinnacle floor.
- Remove the Mediterranean Egg Bake from the oven, permit to chill barely for numerous minutes and garnish as favored with fresh basil or parsley leaves.
- Slice and enjoy while it is hot - on its own or alongside some crusty bread, salad or any side dishes you prefer!
- Make the Mediterranean Egg Bake even more adaptable by including other Mediterranean ingredients like sun-dried tomato, artichoke heart or olives for an exciting and flavorful dish! It will leave a memorable culinary experience in its wake. This flavorful and protein-packed treat is easily prepared ahead of time and re-warmed

once ready to enjoy it at your next brunch gathering!

These mouthwatering brunch ideas celebrate the flavors and traditions of Mediterranean cuisine, creating an enjoyable dining experience at any weekend gathering or special event. By including these recipes into your brunch repertoire, you'll create an impressive and delicious spread to allow your guests to sample all the vibrant and diverse flavors found within Mediterranean cuisine. So gather up your loved ones and experience this Mediterranean-inspired culinary journey together that is sure to leave everyone wanting more!

CHAPTER FOUR: WHOLESOME SALADS AND APPETIZERS

Vibrant and Refreshing Salad Recipes using Seasonal Ingredients

Mediterranean cuisine features salads as an integral component, providing a refreshing and wholesome way to highlight seasonal ingredients in an array of vibrant hues and textures. Packed with fresh vegetables, herbs and a range of textures; Mediterranean salads not only look beautiful but are an exquisite culinary experience too - be it an appetizer or meal, these vibrant recipes will elevate your culinary repertoire while honoring seasonal produce in its abundance!

- **Greek Salad:** Greek Salad is a refreshing and vibrant salad that displays the flavors of Mediterranean cuisine. It has ingredients like crisp vegetables, tangy feta cheese, and a simple dressing. Here's a recipe:

Ingredients:

- 4 medium-sized tomatoes, cut them into wedges
- 1 sliced cucumber
- 1 small thinly sliced red onion
- ½ cup of Kalamata olives
- 1 green bell pepper, cut into thin strips
- 2 tablespoons of extra virgin olive oil
- 1 tablespoon of red wine vinegar
- ½ cup of crumbled feta cheese
- 1 teaspoon of dried oregano
- Salt
- Pepper

Instructions:

- Make an outstanding salad bowl by means of tossing chopped-up tomatoes, cucumber slices, pink onion slices, inexperienced bell pepper strips and Kalamata olives together in a single.
- Mix collectively olive oil, purple wine vinegar, dried oregano leaves, salt and pepper in a small bowl the use of a whisk. It will be used for dressing.
- Pour the dressing over your salad ingredients and gently toss to cover all vegetables evenly.
- Throw some crumbled feta cheese over the salad for added flair!
- Taste and adjust seasoning if necessary, adding additional salt, pepper, or oregano as per personal taste.
- Allowing it to rest for 10-12 minutes allows all the flavors to develop fully and unify into harmony.
- Be sure to give the salad one last gentle stir before serving, to ensure all of the dressing has been evenly dispersed throughout.
- Serve Greek Salad either as a side dish, or pair it with some grilled chicken or shrimp to create a complete meal.

Greek Salad should always be enjoyed fresh and at room temperature for optimal enjoyment. A versatile dish, you can modify this classic salad with ingredients such as cherry tomatoes, capers or herbs such as parsley or mint to enhance its flavors further. Enjoy it as part of any Mediterranean-themed meal or simply as an individual refreshing option!

- **Caprese Salad:** Hailing from Italy's Mediterranean shores, Caprese salad is an incredible Mediterranean feast that celebrates harmony between juicy tomatoes, fresh mozzarella cheese, and fragrant basil leaves. Drizzled with extra virgin olive oil and finished off with sea salt sprinkles for extra seasoning, this dish demonstrates both quality and simplicity in Mediterranean cooking - ideal when tomatoes are in season to add vibrant colors and vibrant flavors to your table!

Here's a recipe:
Ingredients:

- 3-4 sliced ripe tomatoes (vine-ripened)
- Fresh basil leaves
- Extra virgin olive oil
- 8 sliced ounces (225g) of fresh mozzarella cheese
- Balsamic glaze or balsamic vinegar
- Salt
- Pepper

Instructions:

- On a serving platter or individual plates, arrange tomato slices.
- Divide tomato slices among four plates and top each tomato slice with one fresh mozzarella slice.
- Take one basil leaf and carefully tear into smaller pieces before scattering on top of mozzarella for garnish.
- Drizzle extra virgin olive oil over your Caprese Salad to coat every slice of tomato and mozzarella lightly with it.
- Add extra flavor and create beautiful presentations by using balsamic glaze or vinegar as a topping in zigzagging patterns with it.
- Salt and pepper to your tastes; consider that mozzarella cheese may contain sodium that needs to be adjusted accordingly.
- Serve Caprese Salad immediately to experience its fresh taste, whether as an appetizer, side dish or light lunch.

Caprese Salad is an effortless yet elegant dish, designed to showcase the natural flavors and textures of its ingredients. Ideal combinations include juicy tomatoes and creamy mozzarella cheese for optimal results; feel free to customize quantities according to individual preferences for optimal results! Savor this vibrant combination of tastes and textures today!

- **Mediterranean Chickpea Salad:** This protein-packed salad brings chickpeas' nutty sweetness with crunchiness and Mediterranean flair found in cucumbers, cherry tomatoes, red onions, bell peppers and olives to produce an appetizing bite of Mediterranean flair. A zesty dressing made with lemon juice, garlic and extra virgin olive oil adds additional depth of Mediterranean taste while additional ingredients such as feta cheese olives or fresh herbs like parsley or mint enable customization according to personal taste - an enjoyable main or side dish option!

Here's a recipe:
Ingredients:

- 2 cups cooked chickpeas (canned or cooked from dry)
- 1 diced cucumber
- ½ finely chopped red onion
- 1 cup cherry tomatoes, halved
- 1 diced red bell pepper
- ½ cup pitted Kalamata olives, halved
- ¼ cup of diced fresh mint
- Juice of 1 lemon
- ¼ cup of chopped fresh parsley
- 3 tablespoons extra virgin olive oil
- 2 cloves of minced garlic
- 1 teaspoon ground cumin
- Salt
- Pepper

Instructions:

- Combine cooked chickpeas in a large bowl with diced cucumber, diced crimson bell peppers, chopped red onion pieces, cherry tomato halves and Kalamata olive halves for an appealing meal.
- Make the dressing by mixing lemon juice, extra virgin olive oil, minced garlic cloves, ground cumin seeds and floor coriander powder together in a separate small dish along with salt and pepper for seasoning to your own tastes.
- Sprinkle the dressing onto the chickpea and vegetable mix in a large bowl before stirring with a spoon.
- Combine all the dressing ingredients with chopped parsley and mint until everything is thoroughly covered with an even coating.
- Taste and adjust seasoning as necessary by adding more salt, pepper or lemon juice according to individual taste.
- Allow this Mediterranean Chickpea Salad to sit for about 10-15 minutes to allow its flavors to combine fully.
- Before serving, give the salad another gentle toss to redistribute its dressing and herbs evenly throughout its entirety.
- Serve this salad as an aromatic side dish or light meal, fill pita bread pockets with it or top greens with it as desired.

This Mediterranean Chickpea Salad can be prepared and refrigerated ahead of time to allow its flavors to develop further. Feel free to customize it according to your liking by including different ingredients like feta cheese, diced avocado or sun-dried tomato for more vibrant and protein-packed meals! Enjoy this lively yet protein-packed dish!

- **Watermelon and Feta Salad:** Bring out the sweet tastes of summer with this irresistibly refreshing combination of juicy watermelons with creamy saltiness of feta cheese for an irresistibly refreshing summer dish! Fresh mint leaves and balsamic glaze also provide additional savory notes, creating the ultimate summer delight that offers both sweet and savory pleasure on hot summer days!

Here's a recipe on how to prepare it:

Ingredients:

- 4 cups of cubed seedless watermelon
- 1/4 cup of torn fresh mint leaves
- 4 ounces (113g) of crumbled feta cheese
- 2 tablespoons of extra virgin olive oil
- 1 tablespoon of fresh lime juice
- Salt
- Pepper

Instructions:

- Wedge the watermelon cubes into large serving bowl.
- Sprinkle crumbled feta cheese over the watermelon slices for an impressive display.
- Add the crumbled mint leaves to the bowl.
- Whisk the extra virgin olive oil and fresh lime juice together in a small bowl to form the dressing.
- Swirl the dressing through the watermelons, feta, and mint leaves for an irresistibly delicious salad!
- Gently combine all the ingredients together until they are evenly coated with dressing.
- Season to taste with salt and pepper to achieve desired flavors, keeping in mind that feta cheese adds saltiness. Adjust according to desired results.
- Allow the Watermelon and Feta Salad to rest for approximately 10 minutes to allow its flavors to combine.
- Before serving, give the salad one last stir to redistribute its dressing and mint leaves evenly.
- Serve this chilled salad as a refreshing side dish or light appetizer.

Watermelon and Feta Salad is best enjoyed when enjoyed fresh. The combination of sweet watermelons, tart feta cheese, and fragrant mint makes for an irresistibly flavorful salad! Feel free to add additional ingredients such as red onions, cucumber slices or balsamic glaze drizzles to further customize this simple yet satisfying summer dish! Enjoy!

- **Quinoa Tabbouleh:** Tabbouleh is an exquisite classic Levantine salad consisting of bulgur wheat, fresh herbs and vibrant vegetables.

Here's a recipe:

Ingredients:

- 1 cup of quinoa
- 1 large finely chopped cucumber
- 2 large finely chopped tomatoes
- 2 cups of water or vegetable broth

- 1/2 finely diced red onion
- 1 cup fresh parsley, finely chopped
- 1/4 cup of finely diced fresh mint leaves
- Juice of 2 lemons
- 3 tablespoons extra virgin olive oil
- Salt
- Pepper

Instructions:

- Wash quinoa under cold running water in a sieve for at least ten minutes, as this will reduce the bitter taste of quinoa.
- Cover and simmer it for fifteen minutes at medium heat once all the liquid has been absorbed by quinoa.
- Remove from the heat once done to allow time for cooling before freezing or refrigerating!
- Combine cooked quinoa with diced cucumbers, diced tomatoes and crimson onion as well as parsley and mint leaves in one large bowl for smooth mealtime guidance.
- To create the dressing, integrate more virgin olive oils, lemon juice and salt in a small bowl. Pour the dressing onto the quinoa and blend nicely. Make positive the dressing covers all components similarly.
- Add additional salt or pepper, lemon juice if necessary.
- Allow the Quinoa Tabbouleh to rest for 10-15 minutes so the flavors can fully combine. This allows each ingredient to take hold in creating its unique fusion of tastes.
- Give the salad one more good toss before serving and adjust seasoning as necessary.

Serve Quinoa Tabbouleh both as an uplifting main course and side dish for maximum nutrition and energy boost!

Quinoa Tabbouleh can be tailored to any taste by customizing its ingredients such as diced bell peppers or olives, making this salad suitable for potlucks or picnics or adding an eye-catching splash of healthy color and texture to meals at any point in time! Enjoy its vibrant hues and flavors today!

These vibrant and refreshing salad recipes showcase the versatility and abundance of seasonal ingredients used in Mediterranean cooking. By including them into your culinary repertoire, you'll not only celebrate its flavors while providing your body with nutritious yet delectable meals but will also kick start a culinary journey that will leave you craving more colorful salads! So embrace seasonal produce to embark on this enlightening culinary adventure that is sure to leave you craving more vibrant salads!

Flavorful Appetizers to impress Your Guests or Enjoy as Light Meals

Mediterranean cuisine is known for its lively and flavorful appetizers that can elevate any gathering or serve as satisfying light meals. These Mediterranean-inspired appetizers capture the essence of Mediterranean flavors through fresh ingredients, aromatic herbs and bold spices; whether hosting a dinner party or just seeking an exciting light meal these Mediterranean-inspired offerings are sure to please guests and satisfy palates alike!

- **Mezze Platter:** Mezze platters are classic Mediterranean appetizers that provide an array of small bites ideal for sharing and discovering different flavors. Make a colorful platter by layering hummus, tzatziki, tabbouleh, stuffed grape leaves, olives marinated feta cheese and freshly baked pita bread into one colorful arrangement for an engaging dining experience.

Here's the recipe:
Ingredients:

- Assorted olives (for instance, Kalamata or green olives)
- Tzatziki sauce
- Pita bread or breadsticks
- Hummus
- Cherry tomatoes
- Dolmades (stuffed grape leaves)
- Slices of cucumber
- Cubed or crumbled Feta cheese
- Roasted red peppers
- Fresh herbs for garnish (for instance, parsley or mint)

Instructions:

- Arrange the olives and hummus in small bowls on a large plate.
- Add pita or breadsticks to dips.
- Place cherry tomatoes, cucumbers, dolmades (feta cheese), roasted peppers and different ingredients at the platter.
- Garnish your dish with clean herbs.
- Serve the Mezze Platter either as an appetizer, or as part of a Mediterranean unfold.

- **Spinach and Feta Phyllo Triangles:** These bite-sized pastries combine crispy phyllo dough, spinach, and creamy feta cheese in a delightful pastry crust that is then filled with aromatic herbs like dill, parsley and nutmeg for flavoring. Once assembled into triangles they are baked until golden-brown and flaky; making these bite-sized treats both visually appealing and full of delicious flavor a popular choice at gatherings or snacks!

Here's a recipe:
Ingredients:

- Phyllo pastry sheets
- 2 tablespoons of olive oil
- 2 cups of chopped fresh spinach
- 1 cup of crumbled feta cheese
- 1 small finely diced onion
- Salt
- Pepper
- Melted butter or olive oil for brushing

Instructions:

- Pre-warmth the oven to 175degC (350degF).
- Over medium heat, warm olive oil in a saucepan. Sauté the onions in olive oil until they turn out to be translucent.

- Add the spinach and cook dinner it till it wilts. Add salt and pepper.
- Let the spinach calm down.
- Mix the spinach mixture in a bowl with the crumbled feta.
- Spread a thin sheet of phyllo and gently brush it with olive oil or melted butter.
- Brush the top sheet with oil or butter.
- Cut the layers into squares or strips.
- Place a teaspoonful of the spinach-feta combination on one give up of each strip or rectangular.
- Fold the pastry diagonally in a triangle to enclose the filling.
- Continue folding the pastry into a triangle pattern, until the square or strip is folded.
- Repeat this system the use of the closing phyllo and filling.
- Place the triangles full of the filling on a baking tray and brush their tops with melted olive oil or butter.
- Then bake in the oven till golden brown.
- Serve the Spinach and Feta Phyllo Triangles with a Mezze Platter or as a tasty appetizer.

- **Grilled Halloumi Skewers:** Halloumi is an easy and delicious appetizer made of semi-hard cheese with an interesting texture that makes it great for grilling. Simply cut into cubes and thread onto skewers along with cherry tomatoes, bell peppers, and zucchini before grilling until slightly charred and the vegetables tender - the combination of salty halloumi with its slightly tart taste and the smokey-sweet flavors from grilling creates a tantalizing dish sure to please any taste bud.

Here's a recipe:
Ingredients:

- Cut into cubes Halloumi cheese
- Olive oil
- Cherry tomatoes
- Bell peppers (cut into chunks)
- Red onion(cut into wedges)
- Lemon juice
- Fresh herbs (for instance, oregano or basil)
- Skewers
- Pepper
- Salt

Instructions:

- Pre-heat the grill or grill pan.
- Then, thread the cherry tomatoes, bell-pepper chunks, and onion wedges at the skewers.
- To make a marinade, integrate olive oil, lemon, sparkling herbs and salt with pepper in a small bowl.
- Marinade ought to be implemented to all sides of the skewers.
- Place the skewers onto the grill pan or grill preheated.
- Grill the halloumi for 3-four mins on each aspect, or until it's far golden brown. The greens should be barely charred.
- Grilled Halloumi skewers may be served heat with the Mezze platter.

- **Eggplant Caponata:** Eggplant caponata is an irresistibly flavorful Sicilian appetizer, full of Mediterranean flair. Made by sautéing eggplant with onions, bell peppers and tomatoes as well as capers, olives, vinegar and raisins or honey before simmering to bring all its components together and form one luscious spread - serve it alongside crusty bread for an exquisite and rustic starter that showcases eggplant's versatility!

Here's a recipe:
Ingredients:

- 1 large cubed eggplant
- 1 small finely diced onion
- 2 cloves of minced garlic
- 1 can (14 ounces) of diced tomatoes
- 2 tablespoons of red wine vinegar
- 1 tablespoon of capers
- 1 tablespoon of sugar
- ¼ cup chopped of fresh basil
- Olive oil
- Pepper
- Salt

Instructions:

- Heat olive oil in large pan on medium heat.
- Add the minced onion and chopped garlic to the pan, and sauté till the onion will become translucent.
- Add the cubed eggplants to the pan, and prepare dinner them till they are softened and slightly brown.
- Add the capers and sugar to the tomatoes.
- Add salt and pepper according to your flavor.
- Reduce the warmth and simmer the combination for 15-20 minutes to permit the flavors to combo collectively.
- Remove from heat, and put the chopped basil.
- Allow the Caponata to quiet down before serving.
- Serve the Eggplant Caponata as a tasty addition for your Mezze Platter at room temperature.

- **Saganaki:** Saganaki is a Greek appetizer featuring pan-fried cheese, typically created using firm cheese like kefalotyri or halloumi. After being coated in flour or breadcrumbs and pan fried until golden and melty, this treat should be served hot with fresh lemon juice poured over its crispy exterior and soft interior for a truly delightful bite!

Here's a recipe:
Ingredients:

- Olive oil
- 1 block of Greek cheese (for instance kefalotyri, halloumi, or graviera)
- All-purpose flour
- Lemon wedges for serving

Instructions:

- Slice or dice the Greek cheese.
- The cheese need to be dredged in all-cause powder, and any extra flour need to be shook off.
- Heat olive oil over a medium heat.
- Fry the slices of cheese or cubes until they may be golden brown on both facets.
- Remove the cheese from the warmth and drain any extra oil through placing it on a chunk of paper towel.
- Serve Saganaki with lemon wedges.

These flavorful appetizers bring the vibrant and diverse flavors of the Mediterranean right to your table, whether entertaining guests or simply looking forward to a light meal. Their bold flavors, fresh ingredients and alluring aromas will surely impress all those around. So embrace Mediterranean spirit by indulging in these delectable appetizers that will satisfy both you and your guests' cravings.

CHAPTER FIVE: HEARTY SOUPS AND STEWS

Nourishing and comforting soup recipes packed with Mediterranean flavors

Soups and stews hold a special place in Mediterranean cuisine, providing comforting yet nourishing experiences to nourish both body and mind. Packed full of Mediterranean flavors, these hearty bowls of goodness include vegetables, aromatic herbs, and other healthy ingredients - ideal for comforting on cold evenings or nourishing your senses on rainy days alike!

- **Lentil Soup:** Lentil soup is an iconic Mediterranean cuisine dish, providing hearty protein-rich comfort food in one bowl. Created using aromatic vegetables such as onions, carrots, celery and garlic along with cumin and paprika spices this soup provides an exquisite combination of textures that blend with its velvety texture and robust earthiness - add fresh citrus juice or drizzle extra virgin olive oil for extra freshness and enjoy this classic!

Here's the recipe:

Ingredients:

- 1 cup of dried lentils
- 2 diced celery stalks
- 1 diced onion
- 2 diced carrots
- Olive oil for sautéing
- 3 minced garlic clove
- 1 can (14 ounces) of diced tomatoes
- 1 teaspoon of ground coriander
- 1/2 teaspoon of paprika
- 1 teaspoon of ground cumin
- 4 cups of vegetable broth or water
- Salt
- Pepper
- Fresh parsley for garnish

Instructions:

- Wash the lentils beneath cold running water earlier than including chopped celery, carrots and onion (that have all been precut into small chunks for smooth sautéing) together with olive oil in a huge pot over medium-low warmth for 15 to 18 minutes till all have softened in your pot.
- Add cumin, coriander and paprika to the salt and pepper blend before stirring in rinsed lentils along side vegetable broth or water and diced tomatoes into your pot. Give everything another stir!
- Reduce heat after you bring mixture to a rolling boil, cover pot and simmer on low for 30-40 minutes or until lentils become tender. Adjust seasoning if necessary before serving your lentil soup hot with fresh parsley garnishing! You will need: A large pot containing olive oil must first be placed over medium-heat.

- **Tomato and Basil Soup:** Toast Mediterranean flavors in an eye-catching tomato and basil soup! Made with juicy tomatoes, fragrant basil leaves and hints of garlic for maximum brightness. Simmer all of these ingredients until their flavors have come together into something velvety-textured before adding freshly grated Parmesan cheese as garnish for an enjoyable meal experience! Pair this comforting soup with crusty bread slices for the full experience.

Here's the recipe:

Ingredients:

- 2 cans (14 ounces each) of diced tomatoes
- 3 cloves of minced garlic
- 2 tablespoons of tomato paste
- 1/4 cup of heavy cream (optional)
- 1 diced onion
- 4 cups of vegetable broth
- 1/4 cup of diced fresh basil leaves
- Salt
- Pepper
- Olive oil for sautéing

Instructions:

- Add the minced onions and garlic to a pot, sautéing until translucent before mixing in tomato paste for one minute before stirring in tomato dices with juice (if applicable) into the mix for full absorption.
- Reduce heat after brining mixture to rolling boil; cover and allow simmer for 15-20 minutes before pureeing the soup with either an immersion blender, regular blender, or both. Puree soup using either one and return chopped basil back into pot before pureeing again using immersion or regular blender if desired for creamier texture; season to your taste using salt and pepper according to desired effect.
- Heat the soup over low heat until all components have reached desired temperatures, then serve hot. This tomato and basil soup dish makes an unforgettable holiday centerpiece!

- **Fisherman's Stew (Zuppa di Pesce):** This hearty seafood stew hails from the shores of the Mediterranean. Packed full of fresh seafood including fish, shrimp, clams and mussels in an aromatic tomato and herb broth with aromatic spices such as saffron for an unforgettable Mediterranean flavor - this Fisherman's Stew serves as testament to Mediterranean culinary expertise as well as maritime flavors alike.

Here's a recipe:

Ingredients:

- 1 pound mixed seafood (for instance, shrimp, mussels, clams)
- 1 chopped onion
- 1 can (14 ounces) diced tomatoes
- 2 cups of fish or seafood broth
- 2 cloves of minced garlic
- ½ cup of white wine
- 2 tablespoons of tomato paste
- 1/4 cup of chopped fresh parsley
- 1/4 cup of diced fresh basil
- 1/4 teaspoon of red pepper flakes
- Pepper
- Salt
- Olive oil for sautéing

Instructions:

- Add tomato paste and cook for another minute, seasoning as desired with salt and pepper to achieve optimal results.
- Reduce heat to allow flavors to combine and cover saucepan for 15 minutes of simmering uncovered before uncovering (15-20 min should do!). When all seafood has cooked fully and mussels/shellfish have opened up, adjust seasoning as necessary with red pepper flakes as desired; finally garnish it all off with fresh herbs to finish it off!

- **Greek Lemon Chicken Soup (Avgolemono):** This traditional Greek dish combines chicken, rice and an irresistibly velvety lemon-egg sauce into one delicious bite! Comforting yet refreshing at the same time, its bright citrus tang helps cut through any richness in the broth while the silky texture and depth of flavor from eggs create an irresistibly velvety lemon-egg sauce - adding fragrant touches like fresh dill for an aromatic experience - providing soothing nourishment on colder days or whenever needed!

Here's the recipe:
Ingredients:

- 4 cups of chicken broth
- 3 big eggs
- 1/2 cup of shredded cooked chicken
- 1/4 cup of uncooked white rice
- Juice of 2 lemons
- Salt
- Pepper
- Fresh dill for garnish

Instructions:

- Bring chicken broth to a rolling boil in a large pot before adding cooked chicken and uncooked rice, reducing heat as necessary, and simmering until all tasks have been accomplished - about 15-20 minutes should do.
- Whisk lemon juice and eggs together in a large bowl; continue whisking while slowly adding broth into this mix to temper the eggs so they won't curdle in your hot soup. Pour this egg-lemon mixture back into your pot while continuing to whisk continuously.
- Continue to cook the soup over low heat while stirring frequently for another five minutes or until slightly thickened, or the desired texture has been achieved. Feel free to season to your own taste as desired before taking out of heat and serving!

These hearty Mediterranean soup recipes showcase an abundance of delectable flavors and nutritious ingredients, providing comforting culinary experiences to satisfy cravings on cold winter days and warm the belly. Sip in Mediterranean soups and stews while their aromatic Mediterranean charm warms you from within.

Satisfying Stews featuring Legumes, Vegetables and Lean Proteins

Mediterranean cuisine is widely known for its flavorful stews combining legumes, vegetables and lean proteins into satisfying and delicious comforting dishes with Mediterranean flair. Perfect for dinner on a chilly evening or a comforting meal to warm the soul - Mediterranean inspired stews will satisfy both taste buds and appetite alike.

- **Chickpea and Vegetable Stew:** This vegetarian stew honors Mediterranean's devotion to legumes and greens with the aid of pairing smooth chickpeas with seasonal produce like carrots, tomatoes, zucchini and bell peppers in an invitingly flavorful broth that boasts aromatic spices like cumin, paprika and coriander for optimum flavor and delight! Perfect for both vegetarians and meat eaters alike!

Here's a recipe:

Ingredients:

- 1 can (14 ounces) of drained chickpeas
- 1 onion, chopped
- 2 cloves garlic, minced
- 2 carrots, chopped
- 2 celery stalks, chopped
- 1 bell pepper, chopped
- 1 zucchini, chopped
- 1 can (14 ounces) diced tomatoes
- 4 cups vegetable broth
- 1 teaspoon ground cumin
- 1 teaspoon ground coriander
- 1/2 teaspoon paprika
- Salt
- Pepper
- Olive oil for sautéing
- Fresh parsley for garnish

Instructions:

- Begin by heating olive oil over medium heat in a large pot, before stirring in minced onion and garlic for two to three minutes until translucent, before gradually mixing in celery, zucchini, bell peppers, carrots and celery leaves (optional!). Simmer for approximately one more minute for vegetables to soften.
- Combine cumin, coriander and paprika together with salt and pepper before stirring in chickpeas that have been washed, diced tomatoes with their juice, vegetable broth and vegetable bouillon directly to a pot. Bring everything back up to temperature before continuing the recipe.
- Reduce heat after you bring mixture to a rolling boil and cover pot to simmer for 20-25 minutes or until all vegetables are softened. Adjust seasoning as necessary - serve warm garnished with fresh parsley!

- **Italian White Bean and Kale Stew:** This Tuscan-stimulated stew pairs creamy white beans with nutritious kale for an irresistibly scrumptious revel in! Simmered collectively with garlic, onions, tomatoes and aromatic herbs along with rosemary and thyme for maximum comfort - drizzle extra virgin olive oil over for added indulgence!

Here's a recipe:

Ingredients:

- 2 cans (14 ounces each) of drained white beans
- 1 chopped onion
- 3 cloves of minced garlic
- 2 diced carrots
- 2 diced celery stalks
- 4 cups vegetable broth
- 1 can (14 ounces) diced tomatoes
- 2 cups chopped kale
- 1 teaspoon dried oregano
- 1 teaspoon dried thyme
- Salt
- Pepper
- Olive oil for sautéing
- Grated Parmesan cheese for serving (optional)

Instructions:

- Under medium heat, add olive oil to a huge pot on medium-low. Once hot, upload minced onion and garlic; sauté until obvious earlier than stirring in celery, carrots, dried oregano, dried thyme as well as seasoning all of it with salt and pepper for additional flavor!
- Mix collectively white beans (drained and rinsed), diced tomatoes with their juice, and vegetable broth in a pot until all additives have been calmly dispersed. Bring to a rolling boil on high before turning down to low and simmering with lid in place for 15 minutes before taking an initial peek!
- Add the chopped Kale to the pot. Cook, covered, for another 5-10 minutes or until Kale is tender and has begun to wilt, making any necessary seasoning adjustments as necessary. It is then best served warm as is optionally garnished with grated Parmesan for serving!

- **Greek Lamb Stew (Kleftiko):** Kleftiko is an irresistibly pleasant conventional Greek lamb stew made by way of slowly roasting succulent meat marinated with garlic, lemon juice and fragrant herbs like oregano and thyme until its meltingly tender meat emerges. After sealing with parchment paper or foil to fasten in flavors earlier than roasting until meltingly tender meat emerges; growing an impressive yet delectable stew!

Here's a recipe:

Ingredients:

- 2 pounds lamb shoulder or leg (cut into chunks)
- 1 diced onion
- 4 cloves of minced garlic
- 2 diced carrots
- 2 potatoes (peeled and chopped)
- 1 can (14 ounces) diced tomatoes
- 1 cup vegetable or chicken broth
- 1 tablespoon of dried oregano
- 1 tablespoon of dried rosemary
- Juice of 1 lemon
- Salt
- Pepper
- Olive oil for sautéing

Instructions:

- Preheat the oven to 325degF and heat olive oil in an ovenproof large pot or Dutch Oven over medium-low heat, before adding minced onion and garlic before sautéing the onions until translucent.
- Add lamb pieces and brown them on all sides before stirring in carrots and potatoes with seasoning such as salt, pepper, oregano, and rosemary sprigs seasoned accordingly. Next add tomato dice (with juice) into vegetable or chicken broth before stirring to mix thoroughly before covering your pot and simmering gently for several hours or more until desired doneness has been reached.
- Cook the lamb for approximately 2 hours in an oven until it becomes soft enough to easily shred, at which time your stew should be ready to be enjoyed - adjust seasoning if necessary, and serve hot with crusty bread!

CHAPTER SIX: MEDITERRANEAN SEAFOOD DISHES

Seafood Recipes Showcasing the richness of Mediterranean Coastal Cuisine

The Mediterranean region is famed for its abundance of seafood and coastal communities who have embraced it in their cuisine for centuries. From succulent fish to plump shellfish, the Mediterranean coastline provides an abundance of flavors which have inspired an impressive variety of seafood dishes combining freshest catch with aromatic herbs, vibrant vegetables and Mediterranean flair to showcase Mediterranean coastal cuisine's wealth. Come explore a culinary journey which celebrates all that the ocean provides and coastal culture has to offer!

- **Grilled Mediterranean Sea Bass:** Grilling is an iconic method of Mediterranean cuisine and works to perfectly elevate the delicate flavors of sea bass. This elegant yet simple dish showcases freshness of the fish by seasoning it with herbs such as thyme, rosemary and oregano, along with extra virgin olive oil for extra moisture and smokiness. When served alongside fresh salad or roasted vegetables it provides an exquisite coastal Mediterranean dining experience!

Here's a recipe:
Ingredients:

- 4 sea bass fillets
- 2 tablespoons of olive oil
- 1 teaspoon of dried oregano
- 2 cloves of minced garlic
- Juice of 1 lemon
- Salt
- Pepper
- Fresh parsley (for garnish)
- Fresh lemon wedges (for serving)

Instructions:

- Prepare a medium high heat grill. In a small dish, combine olive oil with minced garlic and lemon juice as well as salt, pepper, and dried oregano; season to your own liking with additional spices if necessary.
- Pour this marinade over sea bass fillets evenly to evenly coat all parts; allow marinating time of 15-20 minutes before refrigerating or grilling as per recipe directions.
- Place sea bass fillets onto an already heated grill. Remove them from their marinade, and grill for approximately 4-5 minutes per side or until cooked thoroughly, before transferring onto a serving plate and garnished with lemon wedges and parsley as instructed below.

- **Paella:** Originating in Spain's coastal regions, paella is an irresistibly flavorful rice dish combining seafood with aromatic saffron-infused grains. Traditional Valenciana paella features an assortment of seafood including shrimp, prawns, clams, and mussels, squid along with bell peppers and peas as well as vegetables such as bell peppers. All the different flavors marry perfectly together creating an unparalleled Mediterranean dining experience! Garnish it off with lemon wedges for the full experience!

Here's the recipe:
Ingredients:

- 1 pound shrimp (peeled and deveined)
- 1 pound mussels (cleaned)
- 1 pound of chicken thighs (bone-in and skin-on)
- 1 chopped onion
- 1 chopped bell pepper
- 2 cloves of minced garlic
- 2 cups Arborio or Valencia rice
- 4 cups chicken or vegetable broth
- 1 can (14 ounces) of diced tomatoes
- 1 teaspoon smoked paprika
- ½ teaspoon saffron threads
- Salt
- Pepper

- Olive oil for cooking
- Fresh parsley for garnish
- Lemon wedges for serving

Instructions:

- Heat olive oil over medium heat in a shallow paella pan and fry chicken thighs on both sides until browned before setting them aside to rest. After that, sauté bell peppers, onion, and minced garlic minces together in this same pan until all vegetables have softened completely - about 15 to 30 minutes depending on size of vegetables in pan.
- Stir together the rice, diced tomato with juice, smoked paprika and saffron until combined; toast for approximately one minute then coat in spices before pouring vegetable or chicken broth and simmering.
- Cover and prepare dinner chicken thighs for 20 minutes till all liquid has been absorbed by using the rice, or until all liquid has been used up with the aid of different substances consisting of mussels and shrimp. Add mussels and shrimp; maintain to cover and cook for 5-10 extra minutes or till mussels have opened and shrimp becomes pink.
- Take it off of the heat, allow it to relaxation a few minutes, and serve your Paella with lemon wedges and clean parsley garnishes for garnish.

- **Sicilian-Style Grilled Swordfish:** Swordfish is a staple of Mediterranean cuisine, and Sicilian-style grilled swordfish is an exceptional example of its distinctive flavors. Marinated in an assortment of olive oil, lemon juice, garlic and fresh herbs like parsley and mint before being grilled perfectly to juicy perfection for maximum flavor and zesty goodness. A signature touch from Sicily comes from topping this juicy treat with vibrant salsa Verde made with capers olives herbs drizzled with extra virgin olive oil - a true testament of Sicily's coastal culinary history!

Here's a recipe:
Ingredients:

- 4 swordfish steaks
- 2 tablespoons of lemon juice
- 2 tablespoons of olive oil
- 2 cloves of minced garlic
- 1 tablespoon chopped fresh parsley
- Salt
- Pepper
- Lemon wedges for serving

Instructions:

- Start by warming your grill on medium excessive heat before pre-heating with this recipe.
- Combine olive oil, parsley leaves, minced garlic cloves, salt and pepper in a small mixing bowl before pouring onto swordfish steaks placed in shallow dish.
- Be sure to coat evenly. Allow this step to marinate among 15-20 minutes before enjoying!
- Put steaks onto a preheated grill after taking them out of their marinade, and cook 4-6 minutes on both aspects, or until cooked and flaking effortlessly with a fork. Transfer onto serving plates. For maximum standard results serve along lemon wedges.

- **Moroccan Spiced Grilled Prawns:** Moroccan cuisine brings its distinctive flavors and spices to the world of seafood with dishes like Moroccan Spiced Grilled Prawns. Marinated in a mixture of cumin, paprika, cinnamon, garlic, lemon juice and other warm spices like cumin paprika cinnamon as well as garlic lemon juice they are then grilled until their prawns attain a tantalizing char and fragranced aroma; pair these tasty morsels with either couscous or Moroccan salad for an unforgettable seafood experience!

Here's the recipe:
Ingredients:

- 1 pound big prawns (peeled and deveined)
- 2 tablespoons of olive oil
- 2 cloves garlic (minced)
- 1 teaspoon ground cumin

- 1 teaspoon ground coriander
- 1/2 teaspoon ground paprika
- 1/4 teaspoon ground cinnamon
- Salt
- Pepper
- Lemon wedges (for serving)
- Fresh cilantro (for garnish)

Instructions:

- Begin by preheating your grill to medium heat. Next, in a small mixing bowl combine olive oil with minced garlic and floor cumin before seasoning it with floor coriander seeds, ground coriander stalks, cinnamon powder, floor cumin seed as well as ground coriander leaves for extra seasoning purposes.
- Apply a skinny coating of marinade lightly to every shrimp for your marinate, and allow to marinate for 15-20 minutes before heating your grill and placing your shrimps onto it for 2-3 minutes per facet until opaque and pink in coloration, or till opaque and crimson in hue.
- After grilling has completed, transfer cooked prawns without delay onto a serving plate before devouring! Garnish the dish with sparkling cilantro leaves and lemon wedges to finish its look.

These seafood recipes encapsulate the spirit of Mediterranean coastal cuisine, highlighting its abundance of ocean flavors. From grilling fresh fish, making hearty paella or enjoying vibrant seafood salad, these dishes allow you to taste and appreciate all that the Mediterranean coastline has to offer. So embrace its flavors, and let these recipes transport you directly back to its sun-kissed shores.

Tips for Selecting and Preparing Seafood in order to Achieve Maximum Flavor and Texture

When it comes to Mediterranean seafood dishes, selecting and preparing it properly is of utmost importance for optimal flavor and texture. The Mediterranean region is well known for its fresh and abundant seafood offerings; by following a few simple guidelines you can ensure your dishes truly shine! From selecting appropriate seafood items to understanding proper cooking techniques here are some helpful hints that can maximize your seafood culinary adventures.

- **Purchase Fresh Seafood:** Fresh seafood is of utmost importance when selecting a meal, so look for vibrant and glossy fish with clear eyes, firm flesh, and an aromatic scent of the sea. When shopping for seafood it is wise to purchase from reliable fishmongers or markets with high turnover in order to guarantee yourself the freshest catch available. Furthermore, consider opting for sustainably sourced options which support responsible fishing practices while protecting marine ecosystems.

- **Acquaint Yourself With Mediterranean Seafood Varieties:** Explore the variety of Mediterranean seafood available. This includes white fish like sea bass and cod as well as shellfish like prawns, clams and mussels that each has their own distinct flavors and textures that you should know in order to select appropriate ingredients for your dish and achieve an appealing flavor profile.

- **Proper Storage:** Once you've purchased seafood, it is important that it is stored successfully to preserve its freshness. Refrigerate at 32 to 39 levels Fahrenheit (zero-4 Celsius). Alternatively, keep it on ice in an airtight box to save it from bacteria increase and to experience its height of flavor and excellence.

- **Preparing Seafood:** When coping with seafood for training, it's important that it's treated delicately to preserve its delicate texture. Rinse below bloodless water to get rid of dirt or debris before patting dry with paper towels. Fish fillets or complete fish may additionally require pin bones being extracted the use of tweezers; shellfish might also require scrubbing away any grit from its shell floor - remember to be gentle during the procedure to keep away from making its flesh look unpleasant.

- **Enhancing Flavor with Marinades and Seasonings:** Marinating seafood can bring depth and complexity to your dishes, adding depth of flavor from citrus juice, olive oil, garlic cloves, fresh herbs and spices. Allow it to marinate at least 30 minutes - any longer may damage its texture!

- **Appropriate Cooking Techniques:** The Mediterranean region boasts an array of seafood-cooking techniques. Grilling, baking, poaching and pan-searing are popular ways of enhancing its natural flavors while protecting its delicate texture. Be careful with timing as too keeping it longer will lead to tough and dry results - keep in mind that seafood continues to cook even after being removed from its heat source! For optimal results and the tenderest results slightly undercooking is preferred to ensure succulent results.

- **Paired with Mediterranean Flavors:** The Mediterranean region is well known for its use of fresh herbs, olive oil, citrus fruits, garlic cloves and aromatic spices like oregano and paprika to add depth and complexity to seafood preparations. You can incorporate these Mediterranean influences into your seafood dishes to elevate their taste! Add freshly chopped parsley basil dill over grilled fish or toss in lemon olive oil dressing or experiment with Mediterranean spices like oregano paprika and saffron for even further depth and complexity!

By following these tips for selecting and preparing seafood, you can elevate the Mediterranean seafood dishes you serve to new levels. By emphasizing freshness, proper handling, and mindful cooking techniques, you'll enjoy seafood that bursts with flavor while remaining tender in texture - an experience reminiscent of Mediterranean coastal cuisine! So visit your local seafood market, embrace its flavors, and embark on a culinary adventure full of delectable sea-inspired creations!

CHAPTER SEVEN: PLANT-BASED MAINS AND SIDES

Flavorful vegetarian and vegan recipes highlighting the abundance of plant-based ingredients

The Mediterranean diet is well-known for its emphasis on fresh, wholesome ingredients. As part of its culinary traditions, Mediterranean cuisine celebrates plant-based ingredients in delicious ways: vibrant vegetables and hearty legumes to aromatic herbs and aromatic spices make up delicious plant-based dishes that showcase Mediterranean culinary magic and make delicious additions to any diet - vegetarian or otherwise! These recipes demonstrate its diversity.

- **Ratatouille:** Hailing from southern France and popularized by Mediterranean cuisine, ratatouille is an aromatic vegetable stew that pays homage to seasonal produce. Boil tomatoes, eggplant, zucchini, bell peppers and onions in broth flavored with herbs such as thyme and basil while leaving each vegetable's individual texture and taste intact for an exquisite and aromatic medley of tender yet aromatic goodness - great as either an entree or side dish alongside crusty bread!

Here's the recipe:
Ingredients:

- 1 diced eggplant
- 1 diced bell pepper
- 1 diced onion
- 2 diced zucchini
- 2 cloves of minced garlic
- 1 teaspoon of dried oregano
- 1 can (14 ounces) of diced tomatoes
- 2 tablespoons of tomato paste
- 1 teaspoon of dried thyme
- Salt
- Pepper
- Olive oil

Instructions:

- Start by using heating olive oil over medium-low heat in a big skillet. Stir in diced onion and minced garlic, sauté until translucent before adding eggplant, zucchini and bell pepper dices - cooking those till their vegetables begin softening slightly.
- Stir collectively diced tomatoes (with their juice), tomato paste, dried thyme and oregano leaves, salt and pepper until everything has blended before turning right down to low heat and protecting for several hours till greens have softened on your liking. Adjust seasoning as essential.
- Serve Hot Ratatouille as an accompaniment or with cooked pasta or rice as the centerpiece of any meal!

- **Lebanese Mujadara:** Mujadara is an elegant Middle Eastern dish that elevates lentil and rice combinations with aromatic spices such as cumin and cinnamon for maximum flavor and satisfaction. In its Lebanese rendition, lentils and rice are cooked together with caramelized onions and fragrant cumin and cinnamon spices - creating a flavorful yet hearty meal! For an added punch of flavor finish with some tart yogurt or lemon juice to give an extra pop.

Here's the recipe:

Ingredients:

- 1 cup of brown or green lentils
- 3 tablespoons of olive oil
- 1 cup of basmati rice
- 2 thinly sliced onions
- 1 teaspoon of round cumin
- Salt
- Pepper

Instructions:

- Clear the lentils under cold running water before draining them.
- Boil 3 cups of water in a large pot with 3 cup-worth of lentils added and cooking for approximately 15 minutes or until partially done before draining off and setting aside.
- Heat olive oil over medium heat in a separate pot and stir in onion slices until they turn caramelized and golden-brown in approximately 15-20 minutes, set aside half of these caramelized onions as garnish before proceeding further with this dish.
- Combine partially cooked lentils, basmati rice, floor cumin seeds, salt and pepper; stirring to ensure even distribution.
- Once at boiling, lessen heat to low, cover it tightly, and simmer for 15-20 minutes, or until both the rice and lentils have come to be fully smooth and absolutely cooked. Remove from the warmth once completed to present the whole thing time to settle earlier than taking in addition steps.
- Serve Mujadara warm, garnishing it with the caramelized onions stored.

- **Falafel:** Middle Eastern "fast food" known as Falafel is typically created by combining chickpeas (or fava beans), fresh herbs, and spices into little patties or balls. It is said that Coptic Christians in Egypt created falafel as a meatless alternative to consume during extended periods of fasting or lent. It is additionally grown in popularity as a vegan choice across the Middle East, in particular in Egypt. In almost any a part of Egypt, you could discover a street supplier promoting falafel, that's the staple meals of the people. Sandwiches stuffed with roasted or fried eggplant slices, tahini sauce, and a heaping supporting of Mediterranean salad are a common manner to revel in this dish.

Here's the recipe:

Ingredients:

- 1 small diced onion

- 1 cup of dried chickpeas
- 1 teaspoon of ground coriander
- 1 teaspoon of ground cumin
- 1/2 cup of diced fresh cilantro
- 1/2 teaspoon of baking soda
- 1/2 cup of diced fresh parsley
- 3 cloves of minced garlic
- Pepper
- Salt
- Vegetable oil

Instructions:

- Soak dry chickpeas in water for 1-24 hours before draining off any excess.
- Utilize a food processor to combine soaked chickpeas, chopped parsley, cilantro leaves and onions as well as minced garlic along with ground cumin and coriander seeds, baking soda, salt and pepper until a coarse paste forms.
- Refrigerating falafel mixture for at least an hour allows its flavors to develop while firming it up as well.
- Warm vegetable oil to 350degF (175degC). An electric deep fryer or large pot should be used to heat vegetable oil up until its temperature reaches 350degF, then shape patties or balls of food and fry at this temperature.
- Carefully place falafel patties or balls into hot oil, and fry until golden-brown and crisp - typically three to five minutes. Remove using a slotted spoon from the oil, placing onto paper towel-lined plates so as to minimize oil absorption.
- Serve falafel as a hot snack in pita bread with tahini sauce and vegetables for an appetizer, snack plate or side salad dish.

- **Greek Gigantes Plaki:** Gigantes plaki is a delicious traditional Greek dish composed of giant beans simmered in a delicious tomato sauce with onions, garlic and aromatic herbs for maximum flavor and protein-packed goodness. Serve it alongside crusty bread for an unforgettable main course experience or as an accompanying side to accompany other Mediterranean delectations!

Here's the recipe:

Ingredients:

- 1 cup dried giant beans
- 1 onion, chopped
- 2 cloves garlic, minced
- 1 can (14 ounces) diced tomatoes
- 2 tablespoons tomato paste
- 1 teaspoon dried oregano
- 1/2 teaspoon ground cinnamon
- Salt
- Pepper
- Olive oil for cooking
- Fresh parsley for garnish

Instructions:

- Start by soaking dried giant beans overnight in water before draining off any extra moisture before beginning cooking in a large pot with boiling water.
- Soak your beans overnight, for approximately 45 to 1 hours until partially cooked before draining off and setting aside for later.
- Heat olive oil on medium low, then sauté chopped onion and minced cloves of garlic till translucent, before including diced tomatoes with their juice, tomato paste, dried oregano leaves, ground cinnamon sticks and any extra seasonings as desired; season with extra salt or pepper as vital.
- Add partly cooked giant beans, along side all other elements, into a saucepan and decrease heat earlier than simmering tightly protected for at the least an hour on low warmth. Adjust seasoning as vital earlier than garnishing your finished dish with fresh parsley leaves for optimum effect!

These flavorful vegetarian and vegan recipes spotlight the abundance of plant-based alternatives found in Mediterranean cuisine. By taking advantage of its abundance of greens, legumes, grains, spices and herbs available, these dishes offer an array of flavors, textures and nutrients. These recipes will inspire anybody attempting a plant-primarily based lifestyle or exploring Mediterranean cooking - whether or not pursuing it full time or definitely wanting to discover what its capacity holds! So accumulate sparkling produce spices herbs together on an adventure that highlights Mediterranean plant-primarily based food's colorful and nutritious features!

Sides and Accompaniments to compliment your main dishes

Mediterranean cuisine goes beyond main dish preparation. Side dishes and accompaniments play an instrumental part in rounding out flavor profiles and nutritional balance of any given meal. Focusing heavily on plant-based ingredients, Mediterranean dining provides an abundance of delectable side dishes ranging from vibrant salads and zesty dips to hearty grains and vegetable medleys - each adding freshness, color, and complexity to any plate while rounding off an exquisite dining experience. Let's discover some of these diverse and delectable side and accompaniment options of Mediterranean cuisine together!

- **Greek Salad:** Greek salad is an iconic Mediterranean side dish, known for highlighting fresh produce at their peak. Combinations of crisp cucumbers, juicy tomatoes, tart Kalamata olives and creamy feta cheese (optional for vegans) combined with red onions and drizzles of extra virgin olive oil and lemon juice creates an irresistibly refreshing salad perfect as an accompaniment for main courses like lamb. Vegan options could replace it with tofu or another substitute cheese option!

Ingredients:

- 4 medium-sized tomatoes, cut them into wedges
- 1 sliced cucumber
- 1 small thinly sliced red onion
- ½ cup of Kalamata olives
- 1 green bell pepper, cut into thin strips
- 2 tablespoons of extra virgin olive oil
- 1 tablespoon of red wine vinegar
- ½ cup of crumbled feta cheese
- 1 teaspoon of dried oregano

- Salt
- Pepper

Instructions:

- Make an outstanding salad bowl by means of tossing chopped-up tomatoes, cucumber slices, pink onion slices, inexperienced bell pepper strips and Kalamata olives together in a single.
- Mix collectively olive oil, purple wine vinegar, dried oregano leaves, salt and pepper in a small bowl the use of a whisk. It will be used for dressing.
- Pour the dressing over your salad ingredients and gently toss to cover all vegetables evenly.
- Throw some crumbled feta cheese over the salad for added flair!
- Taste and adjust seasoning if necessary, adding additional salt, pepper, or oregano as per personal taste.
- Allowing it to rest for 10-12 minutes allows all the flavors to develop fully and unify into harmony.
- Be sure to give the salad one last gentle stir before serving, to ensure all of the dressing has been evenly dispersed throughout.
- Serve Greek Salad either as a side dish, or pair it with some grilled chicken or shrimp to create a complete meal.

- **Roasted Vegetables:** Roasting vegetables brings out their natural sweetness while creating depth of flavor. Mediterranean cuisine boasts an abundance of veggies ideal for roasting; carrots, bell peppers, eggplant, zucchini or potatoes all lend themselves beautifully for this preparation method. Add olive oil for optimal drenching then finish by tossing with herbs like rosemary or thyme before roasting to achieve caramelized edges and tender interiors for satisfying side dish pairings with an array of Mediterranean main courses.

Here's the recipe:
Ingredients:

- 2 tablespoons of olive oil
- Assorted vegetables (for instance, bell peppers, zucchini) chop them into bite-sized pieces
- Herbs or spices of your choice (optional)
- Salt
- Pepper

Instructions:

- Preheat the oven to 425degF (220degC). In a large bowl, mix cut vegetables with olive oil, salt, pepper and any additional desired herbs or spices before spreading out on an aluminum or parchment foil-lined baking sheet for even cooking results.
- Roast vegetables for 20-30 minutes, until tender and lightly browned, stirring once or twice during this process. Remove from oven and serve hot as side dishes or as the basis of other recipes.

- **Hummus and Dips:** No Mediterranean meal would be complete without its share of delicious dips! Hummus is an iconic region staple, featuring creamy chickpea puree blended with tahini, garlic, lemon juice, olive oil and other flavors for an irresistibly creamy protein-rich dish to pair perfectly with warm pita bread or raw vegetables. Baba Ganoush features roast eggplant covered in tahini garlic lemon juice olive oil which delivers an irresistibly smoky and satisfying bite while Tzatziki offers refreshing cool relief as an addition. These delectable dips add depth and complexity to meals while making great sides or spreads between sandwiches or wraps!

Here's the recipe for hummus:

Ingredients:

- 3 tablespoons tahini
- 1 can (15 ounces) of drained chickpeas
- 3 tablespoons fresh lemon juice
- 2 cloves garlic (minced)
- 2 tablespoons olive oil
- Salt to taste
- Water (as needed for desired consistency)
- Olive oil, paprika (Optional toppings)

Instructions:

- In a food processor, combine chickpeas, tahini, lemon juice, minced garlic, olive oil and salt into an even texture and creamy consistency.
- If it remains too thick after processing has taken place, gradually add water while continuing until desired results have been reached.
- Adjust the seasoning as necessary by adding salt, lemon juice or garlic as necessary. Transfer hummus to serving bowl and drizzle olive oil over it as an addition for flavor and garnishing purposes - try topping off with paprika, chopped fresh herbs or sesame seeds for additional flair and style!
- Serve Hummus with pita bread and raw vegetables as an easy dip or spread for sandwiches or wraps.

For dips:

- Tzatziki Dip: Combine Greek Yogurt, Grated Cucumbers, Minced Garlic, Fresh Dill Leaves, Lemon Juice, Salt & Pepper in a mixing bowl until all flavors meld before refrigerating before refining for at least 6-8 hours prior to refrigerating and serving. Roasted Red Pepper Dips (RRPD). Mix roasted red peppers, garlic, olive oil, lemon juice, cumin, paprika, salt and pepper until everything is evenly blended together and season according to taste.
- Baba Ganoush: To create Baba Ganoush, roast eggplant until soft before scooping out its flesh to combine with tahini, garlic cloves, lemon juice, olive oil cumin salt and pepper until you achieve an even consistency. Refrigerate before chilling to enjoy this treat!
- Salsa Verde: Combine fresh herbs like parsley, cilantro and basil together with garlic, lemon juice, olive oil, capers (optional), anchovy fillets (if using), salt and pepper until everything is evenly blended.

Mediterranean cuisine provides an abundant range of plant-based sides and accompaniments that add an extra delicious flourish to any meal, such as refreshing salads and zesty dips; hearty grains; roasted vegetables - to name but a few! If you are a vegan or simply trying to incorporate more plant-based meals into your diet, Mediterranean sides and accompaniments offer an ideal balance of flavors, textures, nutrients. Discover its rich culture while appreciating seasonal produce; all this to enhance your dining experience with Mediterranean dining and its delectable plant-based sides!

CHAPTER EIGHT: POULTRY AND MEAT FAVORITES

Delicious and Healthy Recipes Featuring Poultry and Lean Meats

Mediterranean cuisine encompasses an incredible diversity of tastes and ingredients. Although known for its emphasis on fresh produce, Mediterranean dishes also embrace poultry and lean meats - from succulent roast chicken to tender grilled lamb dishes - for optimal balance of taste, nutrition and culinary satisfaction. Drawing upon this vibrant culinary tradition of the region's vibrant culinary traditions, let's discover delicious yet healthy recipes featuring poultry or lean meats in Mediterranean cuisine!

- **Tuscan Herb Roasted Turkey Breast:** Experience Tuscany's rustic charm with our latest recipe—Tuscan Herb Roasted Turkey Breast! This dish celebrates Italian countryside flavors; turkey breast is marinated in an aromatic mixture of olive oil, garlic cloves, fresh rosemary sprigs and thyme leaves combined with white wine to produce an irresistibly succulent and aromatic dish! Served alongside roasted vegetables, creamy polenta and flavorful pan jus for an unforgettable Mediterranean feast!

Here's the recipe:

Ingredients:

- 1 bone-in turkey breast (approximately 5-6 pounds)
- 4 cloves of garlic (minced)
- 2 tablespoons olive oil
- 2 tablespoons Tuscan herb seasoning (or a combination of dried herbs like rosemary, thyme)
- 1 lemon (juiced and zest grated)
- Salt
- Pepper

Instructions:

- Parsley, rosemary, sage, lemon zest, fennel seeds, cayenne pepper, and garlic are combined with 3 tablespoons of oil. Season the entire turkey using salt and pepper by rubbing it all over. Put in a covered shallow baking dish made of nonreactive material. Put it in the fridge for at least four hours (or overnight).
- Set oven temperature to 375. Give the turkey 30 minutes to come to room temperature. Drop the herbs in the pan. Make turkey rolls.
- Wrap with pancetta, then tie with some kitchen twine and return to the pan. Sprinkle with the pepper and the last tablespoon of oil.
- Cook for about one and a half hours, or until an instant-read thermometer put into the turkey's thickest part reads 160 degrees.
- If you want grapes, you can add them to the pan in the final 20 minutes. Place turkey on a chopping board and let aside to rest for 20 minutes.
- Put the juices from the pan in a basin and set them aside for the roasted potatoes. Put the pan on the stove and heat it over medium heat.
- Toss in the wine and reduce it by half while stirring. Bring stock to a boil, then stir in.
- Turn the heat down and let it simmer until it thickens a little.
- Mix with salt and pepper, then stir in finely diced rosemary.

- Turkey should be sliced and served on a dish. Pan sauce seasoned with herbs and a little vinaigrette.

- **Grilled Moroccan Spiced Lamb:** Moroccan cuisine is known for its exotic flavors and fragrant spices, and lamb takes center stage when it comes to lean meats like pork or lamb. A delicious Moroccan spiced lamb recipe showcases how Mediterranean cuisine elevates even basic ingredients - like marinating it with cumin, coriander, paprika and cinnamon spices alongside garlic lemon juice olive oil - creating an irresistibly succulent and fragrant dish which pairs nicely with side of couscous, roast vegetables or yogurt sauce for serving it alongside.

Here's a recipe for Grilled Moroccan Spiced Lamb:

Ingredients:

- 2 pounds lamb chops or lamb leg steaks
- 2 tablespoons of olive oil
- 2 tablespoons Moroccan spice blend (or a mixture of ground cumin, coriander)
- 2 cloves garlic (minced)
- Juice of 1 lemon
- Salt
- Pepper

Instructions:

- In a mixing bowl, integrate olive oil with minced garlic, ground cumin, ground coriander, ground paprika, cinnamon sticks, ground ginger roots and floor turmeric plus lemon juice as well as salt and pepper until you attain an aromatic marinade for chicken or red meat skewers. Mix thoroughly.
- Put lamb chops or loin into a shallow dish or zip-pinnacle bag and pour your desired marinade over them frivolously, massaging to make certain an even distribution. Refrigerate at least 2 hours (preferably overnight) so the flavors have time to penetrate into your meat and penetrate its fibers.
- Preheat the grill over medium-excessive heat.
- Be sure to check out and oil all components of the grates so you can save you your lamb from turning into sticky for the duration of grilling.
- Remove your marinated lamb from the fridge and allow it to return up to room temperature, as a minimum half-hour, before grilling to make certain even cooking. This is essential in creating even effects!
- Put lamb chops or loin right into a shallow dish or zip-top bag and pour your favored marinade over them calmly, massaging to ensure an even distribution. Refrigerate at least 2 hours (ideally in a single day) so the flavors have time to penetrate into your meat and penetrate its fibers.
- Preheat the grill over medium-high warmness. Be positive to check out and oil all components of the grates so you can prevent your lamb from turning into sticky during grilling.
- Remove your marinated lamb from the fridge and permit it to return as much as room temperature, as a minimum half-hour, before grilling to ensure even cooking. This is vital in developing even outcomes!
- Place the lamb onto a preheated grill and cook for approximately 4-6 minutes per side depending on its thickness and desired doneness level. Flip half way through cooking time to ensure even results.
- Once the lamb reaches your desired degree of doneness, remove from the grill and allow it to rest for several minutes so its juices can redistribute within.
- Slice your Grilled Moroccan Spiced Lamb and garnish it with freshly chopped cilantro or parsley for added

freshness and visual appeal.

Serve the grilled lamb as an entree alongside couscous, grilled vegetables or refreshing salad. For additional flavor you could drizzle lemon juice or yogurt sauce onto it to complete this satisfying dish.

- **Greek-Style Grilled Chicken Souvlaki:** Souvlaki is an iconic Greek dish and the epitome of Mediterranean delicacies' ability to transform chicken into an irresistibly flavorful revel in. Chicken breast is marinated in olive oil, lemon juice, garlic and various Greek herbs including oregano and thyme earlier than being skewered and grilled to succulent perfection. Experience with heat pita bread, Tzatziki sauce and Greek salad for the first-rate meal ever.

Here's the recipe:

Ingredients:

- 1.5 pounds boneless, skinless chicken breasts (cut into cubes)
- ¼ cup of olive oil
- ½ teaspoon of salt
- 1 tablespoon dried oregano
- 2 tablespoons fresh lemon juice
- 2 cloves garlic (minced)
- 1 teaspoon dried thyme
- 1 teaspoon paprika
- ¼ teaspoon black pepper
- Wooden skewers, soaked in water for 30 minutes

Instructions:

- Get the marinade ready. Put the garlic, oregano, rosemary, paprika, salt, pepper, olive oil, white wine, lemon juice, and lemon zest (but NOT the dried bay leaves) into the bowl of a small food processor. Mix thoroughly by pulsing.
- Add bay leaves and chicken to a large bowl.
- Add marinade on top. Coat the chicken thoroughly with the marinade by tossing the ingredients together.
- Marinate for 2 hours or overnight in a firmly covered container in the fridge.
- For around half an hour to an hour, soak ten to twelve wooden skewers. Get the Tzatziki sauce and other toppings ready, and get the Greek salad and other sides ready if you're serving them. (Certain accompaniments, like hummus with roasted garlic, may take longer; plan ahead for them).
- When ready, use the prepared skewers to thread the marinated chicken pieces.
- Fire up the grill (or griddle) in the backyard. Lightly oil the grill grate and heat it over medium heat.
- Grill the chicken skewers (or fry them in batches on the griddle) until they are thoroughly cooked through and have an internal temperature of 155 degrees Fahrenheit.
- Skewers should be cooked for about 5 minutes total, with even turning to cook both sides. (Adjust grill heat if required). Lightly coat the meat with the marinade while cooking, and then toss the leftover marinade.
- Chicken should be rested for three minutes after being moved to a serving plate. In the meantime, warm pitas on a grill for a few minutes.
- Prepare the pitas for the grilled chicken souvlaki. Tzatziki sauce on pita, chicken (removed from skewers first, of course), vegetables, and olives.
- The addition of Greek salad, watermelon salad, roasted garlic hummus, or a large Mezze platter to your buffet is entirely up to you.

Mediterranean cuisine provides an assortment of mouthwatering yet nutritious recipes featuring poultry and lean meats, from succulent roast chicken and tender grilled lamb, flavorful turkey cutlets, herb marinated seafood dishes to elevate simple ingredients into satisfying and nutritious dishes. Whether hosting a dinner party or planning weekday family meals, these Mediterranean-inspired poultry and lean meat recipes are certain to tempt both taste buds and bodies alike! So embrace its flavors today, indulge in its culinary treats, and celebrate life a little.

Tips for Cooking Meats to Perfection While Maintaining Juiciness

Mediterranean cuisine is famed for its ability to craft succulent and flavorful meat dishes, from tender kebabs to mouthwatering roast chicken dishes. Crafting juicy yet well-cooked pieces of meat is at the center of Mediterranean culinary traditions; here we explore tips and techniques used in Mediterranean cooking to achieve that balance while keeping their juices intact.

- **Marination:** Marinating meats is an integral step of Mediterranean cooking that adds flavor, tenderness, and juicy textures to dishes. A marinade typically comprises ingredients such as olive oil, citrus juice, vinegar, herbs and spices to achieve this aim; with acids breaking down connective tissues within the meat that result in tender and succulent textures. It is recommended marinating for at least four hours (ideally overnight!) in the refrigerator to achieve best results.

- **Proper Seasoning:** Seasoning meat before cooking is critical to its natural flavors, especially Mediterranean cuisine that features herbs and spices like rosemary, thyme, oregano and basil. While spices such as paprika cumin coriander add warm aromas - that elevate its natural tastes and seal in natural juices for delicious results! Ensure an even coat by applying seasoning evenly around all sides - this step not only adds taste but helps seal in its juices more securely too.

- **Preheating and Resting:** Preheating any cooking surface - whether grill, pan, or oven - to achieve your desired level of sear is key to attaining tender and juicy final product. When properly heated, caramelized crust forms on meat that seals in moisture while simultaneously intensifying flavors. Allowing cooked meat to rest before cutting or serving is also highly important; resting allows its juices to redistribute throughout its body for increased tenderness resulting in juicy final products! Cover it loosely with aluminum foil for 5-10 minutes prior to serving to achieve perfection!

- **Monitoring Internal Temperature:** To make sure meats are cooked to their ideal doneness while maintaining their juiciness, using a meat thermometer is indispensable. With its accurate temperature readings and specific recommendations for different kinds of meat - like chicken at 165F/74C for optimal cooking while medium rare beef should reach 135F (57C), using this handy device can ensure perfect results without overcooking! By adhering to these temperature specifications and following recommended temperatures you can prevent overcooking as well as preserve its juicy goodness!

- **Searing and Slow Cooking:** Searing meat at high heat before slowly slow-cooking it is a technique commonly employed in Mediterranean cuisine, creating caramelized surface flavor in the meat for enhanced savory and rich tastes. After searing, meat can then be slowly simmered at lower temperature so heat penetrates slowly enough so as to maintain moistness and tender texture throughout. This method works particularly well when dealing with tougher cuts of meat that require longer breaking down their collagen layers in order to achieve tender textures.

- **Basting and Moisture Retention:** Basting is another effective technique for keeping meat juicy during its cooking process, using liquid such as marinade, broth or pan drippings as basting fluid at regular intervals during its cook-out to brush over it in an attempt to maintain moisture balance within. Basting can particularly useful when grilling or roasting as direct heat may quickly evaporate its natural juices that keep meat juicy during this step of its journey to our dinner plates.

- **Slice and Serve:** Your method for cutting and serving cooked meat can also impact its juiciness. When dealing with steak or roast, cutting against the grain (perpendicular to muscle fibers) often produces shorter fibers for tendered texture and an optimal outcome. Furthermore, it is vital that slicing occurs right before serving so as to maintain maximum juice retention levels and freshness levels for every serving.

Ultimately, perfect meat preparation while maintaining their juicy goodness lies at the core of Mediterranean cuisine. By following these techniques and tips outlined above, you can unlock their secrets for producing succulent and flavorful dishes - marinating and seasoning to preheating and resting are all vital steps that help ensure meats reach desired doneness while still retaining their juicy properties. So next time you embark on your Mediterranean culinary adventure make sure you remember these tips so you can experience exquisitely-done juicy meat dishes to take your dining experience to new heights!

CHAPTER NINE: IRRESISTIBLE MEDITERRANEAN DESSERTS

Indulgent yet wholesome dessert recipes inspired by Mediterranean flavors

When considering Mediterranean cuisine, many may envision dishes featuring fresh herbs, vibrant vegetables and succulent meats. Yet the Mediterranean region also hosts an impressive range of delightful desserts that balance indulgence with healthy ingredients. In this piece we will dive deeper into this culinary region's offerings to showcase how Mediterranean-inspired desserts create exquisite tastes while remaining health-oriented.

- **Baklava:** Baklava is an iconic Mediterranean dessert with global appeal. Layers of thin phyllo pastry are filled with finely chopped nuts like walnuts or pistachios and sweetened by fragrant syrup made from honey, lemon juice, spices like cinnamon and cloves - creating an irresistibly decadent confection which perfectly captures Mediterranean flavors.

Here's the recipe:

Ingredients:

- 1 package (16 ounces) phyllo dough
- 1 cup of granulated sugar
- 2 cups finely chopped nuts (for instance, walnuts, pistachios)
- 1 teaspoon of ground cinnamon
- 1 ½ cups unsalted butter (melted)
- 1 teaspoon of vanilla extract
- 1 cup of honey
- 1 cup of water
- Additional nuts for garnish (optional)

Instructions:

- Preheat your oven to 350degF (175degC).
- Mix ground cinnamon and chopped nuts collectively in a huge bowl for maximum effect.
- Butter melted in a 9x13 baking dish is set out for melting.
- Apply 8 to 10 sheets of the phyllo dough to the baking dish and brush each sheet with butter melted before placing another one on.
- Overlain your phyllo with generous quantities of the nut mix for maximum impact.
- Repeat steps 4 & 5 until all the nut mix has been used up, then place one more sheet of phyllo on top as the finishing touch.
- Cut your baklava using a sharp knife into square or diamond shapes for easier cutting.
- Bake in an oiled or parchment coated casserole for 45-50 minutes till golden and crunchy.
- As your baklava bakes, integrate sugar, honey, water, vanilla extract and extract in a saucepan and bring to a rolling boil before turning right down to low and simmering for 10-12 minutes until your syrup thickens slightly.
- Once removed from the oven, pour hot syrup at once on top.
- Before serving, allow the baklava to completely cool before decorating with additional nuts as desired.

- **Fig and Ricotta Tart:** Figs are a beloved Mediterranean fruit that are frequently featured in desserts. A fig and ricotta tart combines their sweet juiciness with the velvety richness of ricotta cheese for an exquisite dessert experience. A tart shell is then filled with this velvety mixture made up of sugar, ricotta cheese, vanilla bean extract, sugar, and fresh sliced figs for an eye-catching dish that captures Mediterranean spirit!

Here's the recipe:
Ingredients:

- 1 sheet frozen puff pastry (thawed)
- 1 cup ricotta cheese
- 1 tablespoon honey
- 1 teaspoon vanilla extract
- 6-8 fresh figs (sliced)
- 2 tablespoons chopped pistachios (optional)
- Powdered sugar (for dusting)

Instructions:

- Aim for 200degC (428degF).
- Roll out your puff pastry sheet on a lightly floured surface to fit a tart pan.
- Prick the puff pastry from all sides using a fork.
- Combine ricotta, honey and vanilla extract in a large bowl until everything has been fully mixed together.
- Spread ricotta evenly over the puff pastry.
- Simply arrange the slices of fig over the ricotta cheese mixture and gently press into it with your palms to embed the fruit within its layers of cheese.
- Add chopped pistachios for an additional decorative element if desired.
- Make the pastry golden-brown and puffy by baking in an oven until it reaches desired puffiness.
- Once removed from the oven, allow the dish to cool for several minutes before refrigerating or serving it immediately.
- Just before serving, dust the tart with powdered or granulated sugar for added color and flavor.

- **Pistachio and Honey Baklava:** For something truly unforgettable, look no further. This twist on traditional baklava features layers of flaky phyllo pastry filled with crushed pistachio nuts sweetened by honey for an irresistibly satisfying dessert! With crunchy nuts tangled among sticky honey, Pistachio and Honey Baklava creates an irresistibly delightful treat that is both decadent and filling!

Here's the recipe:
Ingredients:

- 1 ½ cups unsalted butter (melted)
- 1 package of (16 ounces) phyllo dough
- 2 cups finely chopped pistachios

- 1 cup of granulated sugar
- 1 cup of water
- 1 teaspoon vanilla extract
- 1 cup of honey

Instructions:

- Preheat your oven to 350degF or 175degC before you start.
- Mix sugar and pistachios in a bowl until well mixed.
- Butter melted in a 9x13 baking dish is now ready for baking!
- Add 8-10 sheets of the phyllo dough to the baking dish, brushing each sheet with butter melted before placing another.
- Distribute generously the mixture of ground pistachios and sugar on top of the phyllo dough.
- Repeat steps 4 and 5, ending with an added phyllo layer at the top.
- Slice your baklava using a sharp knife into square or diamond shapes for best results.
- Bake in an unpreheated oven for 45-50 minutes until golden-brown and crisp.
- As your baklava bakes, mix sugar, honey, vanilla extract and water in a saucepan and bring to a rolling boil before turning down to low and simmering until its consistency thickens slightly - approximately 10 minutes should do it!
- As soon as it has come out of the oven, drizzle hot syrup onto your freshly-made baklava and enjoy!
- Allow the baklava to completely cool before refrigerating or refining for storage or serving.

- **Orange and Almond Biscotti:** Biscotti is an irresistibly delicious treat when enjoyed alongside coffee or tea, especially this Mediterranean-inspired version with oranges and almonds paired perfectly. Made using almond flour, orange zest, and sliced almonds - you get an aromatic cookie perfect for hot beverages like coffee and tea!

Here's the recipe:

Ingredients:

- 2 cups all-purpose flour
- 1 ½ teaspoons baking powder
- ¼ teaspoon salt
- 2 tablespoons of unsalted butter (softened)
- 2 big eggs
- ½ cup of granulated sugar
- 1 teaspoon vanilla extract
- Zest of 1 orange
- ½ cup chopped almonds

Instructions:

- Preheat the oven to 350degF or 175degC before starting this recipe.
- Mix flour, salt and baking powder in a large bowl.
- Mix sugar and butter until fluffy in a separate bowl.
- Once added, beat each egg thoroughly after adding it before mixing in orange zest and vanilla extract.
- Gradually add the flour mixture to the wet ingredients and combine.
- Fold almonds into batter before dividing evenly and shaping each portion into an 11"x 2" log shape.
- Place the logs onto a baking tray covered with parchment paper earlier than intending with baking.
- Baking time must take approximately 25-30 minutes in an ungreased oven at 400F/200C.
- Once removed from the oven, permit logs to cool for as a minimum 10 to 15 minutes before returning them to their storage packing containers for safekeeping.
- Cut logs into skinny slices - about half of an inch thickness – by using a sharp knife.
- Bake biscotti slices for 10-15 additional minutes or until their crispy and golden-brown hue has fully developed.
- Remove your biscotti from the oven, allowing it to cool on a wire rack before refrigerating for storage purposes.
- After biscotti have set, store in an airtight container to extend their freshness for several days.

Mediterranean-inspired desserts provide the perfect balance of indulgence and healthfulness. Ranging from fresh fruit tarts to nut-filled pastries, Mediterranean-inspired treats celebrate the natural flavors of their Mediterranean region while including nutritious ingredients in each sweet bite. Enjoy almond and orange cakes or Greek yogurt parfait for an irresistibly delightful finish to a Mediterranean feast - enjoy Mediterranean desserts for their richness of flavors and goodness of ingredients; let your taste buds experience something truly delightful.

Tips for incorporating healthier alternatives into traditional desserts

Delight in sweet treats is one of life's great pleasures, and Mediterranean cuisine provides an irresistibly delectable selection. However, if you want something healthier without compromising taste or flavor, there are numerous strategies and techniques for adding healthier elements into traditional Mediterranean desserts. We will explore them.

- **Swapping Refined Sugar for Natural Sweeteners:** Traditional Mediterranean desserts often rely on refined sugar as their sweetener of choice, however there are healthier options like honey, maple syrup or date syrup that offer just a hint of sweetness with added nutrients and distinctive flavor profiles that add complexity and depth to each dessert recipe. Experiment with various natural sweeteners until you find one that best complements its flavors!

- **Use Whole Grain Flour:** In place of refined white flour, consider replacing it with whole grain varieties like whole wheat flour, spelt flour or almond flour which contain more fiber and nutrients for more nutritious desserts. Whole grain flours can be found in various Mediterranean desserts including cakes, cookies and breads without altering their taste or texture.

- **Integrate Nut Butters:** Nut butters like almond or cashew butter make an excellent addition to Mediterranean desserts, adding richness, creaminess and healthy fats while elevating overall flavors. Use some or all of it in place of butter or oil in recipes in order to lower saturated fat content while still achieving moist textures in desserts!

- **Enhance Nutritional Value with Nuts and Seeds:** Mediterranean desserts often feature nuts and seeds as key components, adding delicious crunch while providing essential fats, proteins, vitamins, and essential minerals. Consider including chopped almonds walnuts pistachios into your dessert for additional nutrition as well as delightful texture; for added fiber and omega 3s sprinkle some chia, flax or sesame seeds on top for even greater nutrition value!

- **Celebrate Fresh Fruits:** Mediterranean cuisine celebrates the natural sweetness of fresh fruits, so adding them into desserts is a delicious and nutritious way to enhance both flavor and nutrients. Use seasonal fruits such as seasonal berries, figs, pomegranates or citrus as toppings or fillers and as natural sweeteners in Mediterranean-inspired desserts for maximum impact - they add zesty notes while providing refreshing elements to sweet creations!

- **Yogurt Can Reduce Saturated Fat Content in Desserts:** Mediterranean desserts often feature butter or heavy cream that's high in saturated fat content, for healthier desserts try replacing some or all of this ingredient with Greek or strained yogurt as an ingredient - Greek yogurt's creaminess adds moisture while at the same time decreasing saturated fat levels!

- **Experiment with Spices and Flavorings:** Mediterranean cuisine is famous for its bold and aromatic spices, so adding cinnamon, nutmeg, cardamom or vanilla into dessert recipes can add depth of flavor without resorting to excessive sugar or fat content. Not only can these spices add depth of flavor; they may also offer health advantages like anti-inflammatory properties and improved digestion!

- **Portion Control:** While healthier ingredient substitutions are important, portion control should also be practiced with Mediterranean desserts to maximize enjoyment while not overindulging or feeling guilty about overeating them. By exercising portion control you can still indulge in your sweets without overeating and feeling guiltily indulgent!

- **Take Advantage of Dark Chocolate:** Dark chocolate's high cocoa content makes it a healthier option when making Mediterranean desserts, thanks to antioxidants and lower amounts of added sugar. Incorporate it by melting and drizzling over fruits or nuts before coating with batter for rich chocolate flavors!

- **Experiment with Alternative Dairy Products:** Looking to reduce dairy intake or meet dietary restrictions that prohibit dairy? Luckily there are alternative dairy products out there such as almond, coconut or oat milk as suitable replacements. You could try swapping almond, coconut or oat milks out in dessert recipes instead of cow's milk; their creamy textures provide delicious puddings, custards or ice cream treats!

- **Explore Natural Thickeners:** Mediterranean desserts typically use eggs, cream or gelatin as thickeners; but healthier options exist that can achieve similar effects. Agar-agar (an edible seaweed gelatin alternative), can be used to thicken fruit jellies or puddings while soaked chia seeds form gel-like consistency that allows users to create creamy yet healthier puddings.

- **Choose High-Quality Ingredients:** When creating healthier Mediterranean desserts, choosing quality ingredients is of utmost importance. When possible, use organic or locally sourced fruits, nuts, and grains sourced directly from nature for best results and optimal flavor profiles from Mediterranean regions. By opting for fresh ingredients from nature you will increase the overall nutritional value and enjoy more vivid Mediterranean tastes in each bite of dessert you create!

- **Mindful Baking:** Mindful baking requires being present and aware of all ingredients and techniques involved in the baking process, deepening your relationship with food while making more conscious choices about its preparation and consumption. When baking Mediterranean desserts, take time to appreciate all their flavors and textures while mixing, folding and baking; being mindful allows for greater control of ingredient quantities for healthier desserts that satisfy more palates!

- **Consider Gluten-Free Options:** Those who require gluten free diets have plenty of delicious Mediterranean dessert alternatives available that offer variety while satisfying individual dietary restrictions and needs. Explore gluten-free flours such as rice flour, quinoa flour or buckwheat flour when creating tasty treats that everyone will love - using gluten free options can bring added variety while satisfying multiple diet needs at the same time!

- **Balance Indulgence with Nutritional Value:** While making healthier food choices is certainly beneficial, striking the proper balance between indulgence and nutritional value should also be prioritized. Desserts should only be enjoyed occasionally so instead of completely eliminating traditional ingredients from Mediterranean desserts altogether try decreasing quantities while adding healthier ones into moderation to enjoy Mediterranean desserts with an eye on healthier alternatives - that way you'll still experience their flavors and textures while maintaining an approach that embraces their healthfulness!

By following these tips, you can craft healthier versions of traditional Mediterranean desserts without compromising taste or enjoyment. From baking delicious almond and orange cakes with whole grain flour, or replacing refined sugar with honey drizzles in fruit salad, even simple changes like adding whole-wheat flour can have an enormously positive effect on their nutritional profile. Be creative in the kitchen while trying healthier options, and watch both taste buds and well-being reap benefits of balanced Mediterranean dessert consumption!

Note that adding healthier options into traditional Mediterranean desserts allows you to both appreciate their sweet pleasures while fueling your body with essential nutrition. By replacing refined sugar with natural sweeteners and whole grain flours with reduced saturated fat content (yogurt is great!), including nuts/seeds into recipes and practicing portion control; you can create tasty yet healthier treats! So get creative, gather all your ingredients, unleash your imagination, and embark on an incredible culinary adventure that fuses Mediterranean flavor profiles with more nutritious choices for delicious results!

CHAPTER TEN: 8-WEEK NO-STRESS MEAL PLAN

A Comprehensive 8-Week Meal Plan featuring Mediterranean Recipes

Setting out to adopt a Mediterranean-inspired lifestyle can be both exciting and daunting. Renowned for its abundance of fresh ingredients, vibrant flavors, and myriad health benefits, the Mediterranean diet is known for promoting wellbeing and longevity. To ease into this wholesome way of eating seamlessly, we have put together an 8-week meal plan featuring delectable Mediterranean recipes while simultaneously minimizing stress levels and optimizing nutrition.

Week 1: Beginning the Mediterranean Diet

Our meal plan's first week aims to introduce you to the fundamental principles and flavors of Mediterranean eating. Breakfast options such as Greek yogurt with fresh berries and honey is followed by vibrant salads featuring cucumbers, tomatoes, olives and feta cheese for lunch; followed by dinner dishes such as classic Mediterranean fare such as grilled chicken with lemon herbs served alongside roasted vegetables as a side dish - while snacks like nuts, seeds or fresh fruits help energize you for the rest of the day!

Week 2-3: Investigating Mediterranean Pantry

Weeks 2 and 3 introduce us to the Mediterranean pantry, exploring its key ingredients and using them in various recipes. This includes olive oil, whole grains, legumes, herbs and spices as staples in meals such as homemade granola with Greek yogurt for breakfast; grain bowls featuring quinoa with roasted vegetables topped off with tahini dressing at lunch; Mediterranean-inspired baked fish served alongside whole wheat couscous and sautéed greens at dinnertime!

Week 4-5: Seafood Extravaganza

Weeks 4 and 5 focus on celebrating the coastal flavors of Mediterranean by featuring seafood-centric recipes for breakfast, lunch and dinner. Breakfast may feature smoked salmon and avocado toast while lunch may include shrimp skewers served over mixed greens or even an unforgettable seafood paella packed with mussels, shrimp and calamari! Take this chance to explore all that seafood offers while reaping health benefits associated with omega-3 fatty acids and lean proteins!

Week 6-7: Delectable Vegetarian Dishes

Weeks 6 and 7 feature vegetarian cuisine, taking full advantage of the abundance of plant-based ingredients found throughout Mediterranean cooking. Breakfast features hearty vegetable frittatas or spinach-feta omelets for breakfast; lunches feature Mediterranean-inspired mezze platters including hummus, falafel, tabbouleh and grilled vegetables; while dinner features an eggplant and lentil moussaka with rich tomato sauce and creamy béchamel; these weeks highlight the versatility and deliciousness of plant-based Mediterranean meals!

Week 8: Culinary Adventure

As part of our final meal plan, we encourage you to embark on a culinary adventure by trying new recipes and exploring Mediterranean-inspired fusion cuisine. Breakfast might feature Shakshuka (a savory tomato and bell pepper stew topped with poached eggs). Lunch may include quinoa and roasted vegetable salad with zesty lemon dressing; dinner could include innovative options like grilled halloumi and watermeon skewers that combine sweet and savory tastes!

As part of your 8-week meal plan, we encourage you to embrace all aspects of Mediterranean lifestyle fully. This means savoring meals with family and friends, taking leisurely walks after dinner, and including physical activity into daily life - remember, the Mediterranean diet encompasses more than food alone; it encompasses holistic approaches towards health and well-being.

It is essential to note the following points as you conclude the 8-week meal plan.

- **Important Considerations for Mindful Meal Planning:** Our meal plan recognizes the significance of mindful meal planning. Each week, we offer recipes from across food groups and flavors for a well-balanced and satisfying diet. Furthermore, we take into account portion sizes while encouraging mindful eating practices such as slowing down when eating and listening to our body's hunger/fullness cues.
- **Accepting Seasonal Ingredients:** Our 8-week meal plan places great emphasis on using seasonal ingredients. By including fresh, locally sourced produce into your meals, not only are you supporting local farmers but you are also reaping all of its nutritional and flavorful advantages that each season has to offer - from summer tomatoes and zucchini to winter root vegetables, our meal plan encourages exploring all its bounty!
- **Convenience and Versatility:** At our meal plan, we understand modern lifestyles can be hectic; therefore we provide recipes which are convenient and versatile. With suggestions for batch cooking and meal prepping to save you time during the week. Many of these dishes can easily be modified based on individual tastes or dietary restrictions so everyone can experience Mediterranean flavors!
- **Balancing Macronutrients:** The Mediterranean diet is well known for balancing macronutrients - carbohydrates, proteins and fats - in every meal. Our meal plan ensures you receive adequate amounts of each macronutrient with each meal; for instance breakfast could include whole grain carbohydrates like oatmeal or whole wheat bread with Greek yogurt, eggs or healthy fat sources like nuts or avocado for example. This balanced approach keeps you energized and satisfied all day long!
- **Introduce New Flavors and Techniques:** This 8-week meal plan will introduce you to the rich flavors and techniques associated with Mediterranean cuisine. From using fragrant herbs like oregano and thyme, to adding tart citrus notes and exploring grilling or roasting methods - all will expand your culinary horizons while helping you discover all its unique delights!
- **Sustainability and Mindful Eating:** The Mediterranean diet encourages sustainability through consumption of seasonal, locally sourced ingredients as well as reduced food waste. Mindful eating practices such as focusing on tasting flavors while building positive associations between eating habits and healthy relationships between ourselves and food are encouraged in accordance with these principles.

Our comprehensive 8-week meal plan offers a roadmap for transitioning to a Mediterranean lifestyle while simultaneously minimizing stress and increasing enjoyment. By including fresh ingredients, flavorful herbs and spices, lean proteins, and healthy fats into each dish of this plan, it ensures you experience all of Mediterranean cuisine's health benefits - so put on your apron, stock up your pantry with essentials, and embark on an energizing flavor journey that both nourishes your body while delighting your taste buds - cheers to a healthier and more vibrant future!

Tips for meal prepping, shopping and adapting the plan to your preferences

Engaging in an 8-week meal plan can be an exciting journey towards living a healthier and more holistic lifestyle. The 8-Week No-Stress Meal Plan, featuring Mediterranean dishes, was developed with this goal in mind and provides delicious Mediterranean recipes along with flexibility and personalization features to facilitate this change in lifestyle. Here we will provide essential tips for meal prepping, shopping, and adapting the plan according to individual preference - providing an exciting start in finding your way towards wellness!

- **Meal Prepping Made Easier**

Prep is one of the cornerstones of an 8-week meal plan and should not be daunting or stressful; rather, meal prepping provides you with an effective means to save time, reduce stress, and ensure nutritious meals are readily available throughout your week. Here are a few helpful hints that should make meal prepping much simpler:

- **Plan in Advance:** Take time to carefully consider your meal plan for the week ahead, making a list of recipes you wish to prepare and making an inventory list containing all required items. Doing this will keep things on track and prevent last minute disasters!
- **Batch Cooking:** Consider bulk-cooking certain components that can be easily integrated into various dishes at one time, like roast vegetables, cooked grains and chicken to save both time and effort in your recipes. Roast vegetables can easily be included into several meals by batch cooking them all ahead of time or cooking multiple batches at the beginning of every week with these versatile components - saving both effort and time in doing so!
- **Portion Control:** When meal prepping, be sure to portion out each of your meals into individual containers to aid with portion control and make grabbing meals when on-the-go easier. Consider investing in high quality microwave and freezer safe storage containers for additional ease and comfort.

- **Smart Shopping for Mediterranean Ingredients**

In order to successfully follow an 8-week meal plan, stocking both your pantry and refrigerator with appropriate Mediterranean ingredients is key to its success. Here are a few helpful shopping strategies.

- **Make A List:** Before visiting your grocery store, create a comprehensive shopping list based on recipes for this week that you are planning on cooking and shopping for. Doing this will keep you focused and help prevent making unnecessary purchases. Also be sure to double-check both pantry and fridge beforehand to see if anything similar exists within them already!
- **Shop the Perimeter:** In most grocery stores, fresh produce, meat and seafood sections can be found around the perimeter. Focus on your cart filling it up with seasonal fruit and veggies along with lean proteins like seafood to capture Mediterranean cuisine in its full glory!
- **Read Labels:** When purchasing packaged foods such as canned goods or sauces, be mindful of what goes into them. Look for those with minimal additives, low sodium levels and no added sugars as well as whole grain options such as whole wheat pasta or brown rice over refined ones.
- **Explore Local Markets:** Discover your local farmers' markets or specialty stores offering fresh, local, organic produce for an expanded variety of fresh ingredients and the chance to support small local businesses at once! You could gain access to high-quality ingredients.

- **Customize Your Meal Plan**

Although the 8-week meal plan serves as a general framework for Mediterranean eating, you should adapt it according to your own dietary and personal tastes and needs. Here are a few suggestions on how you can customize it:

- **Modifying Recipes:** Feel free to customize any recipes according to your personal taste preferences or dietary restrictions, by swapping out ingredients or increasing seasoning levels if necessary (if you like spicy foods add extra herbs & spices); for people with food restrictions/allergies make substitutions accordingly; etc.
- **Portion Sizes:** While meal plans provide suggested portion sizes, it's essential that you listen to what works for your own individual body in terms of hunger and fullness cues. If the suggested portions don't satisfy, adjust them as necessary - each person's requirements differ, so finding something that meets them all is vitally important!
- **Flexibility:** Although the meal plan has been created with 8 weeks in mind, you don't need to adhere strictly to it every single day! Feel free to repeat favorite recipes from past weeks, mix-and-match meals from various weeks or add other Mediterranean inspired dishes as necessary. The key is enjoying this process and making it sustainable over time!
- **Experiment and Explore:** Use your meal plan as an entryway into exploring new flavors, ingredients and cooking techniques. Feel free to experiment with various herbs, spices and methods of adding personal flair to the recipes using Mediterranean ingredients and flavors - take this chance to be creative in the kitchen!
- **Flexible Ingredient Selections:** While our meal plan provides specific ingredients for every recipe, you have the flexibility to modify or switch out individual components as per your tastes or dietary restrictions. For instance, if a vegetable or protein source doesn't float your boat, feel free to swap out for another ingredient you prefer and preserve the balance among flavor, textures, and nutrients within each dish.
- **Customizing Seasonings and Spices:** Mediterranean cuisine is known for its flavorful combination of herbs, spices, and condiments that create its distinctive fragrances and aromas. Feel free to adjust seasonings used in recipes according to your personal taste. For bolder flavor profiles you may wish to increase herb or spice amounts or try different combinations; conversely if milder tastes appeal more you can decrease them accordingly.
- **Dietary Restrictions and Allergies:** When catering to specific dietary restrictions or allergies, meal planning must adapt accordingly. For instance, those following gluten-free diets should substitute grains such as wheat or barley with gluten-free alternatives like quinoa or brown rice; similarly if there is dairy allergy involved it's essential that nondairy alternatives like almond milk or coconut yogurt be found which will still maintain the integrity of Mediterranean cuisine dishes while still satisfying this criteria.
- **Portion Control and Energy Needs:** Although meal plans provide suggested portion sizes, it's essential that they take your individual energy requirements and appetite into account. For example, physical activity or faster metabolism might necessitate increasing portion sizes or adding snacks in order to meet nutritional requirements; alternatively if trying to lose weight you might require decreasing portion sizes accordingly; listen to what feels right to ensure a fulfilling and energetic day ahead!
- **Variety and Experimentation:** While this 8-week meal plan aims to introduce you to an assortment of Mediterranean recipes, don't be intimidated to add your favorite fruits, vegetables or proteins into recipes for added variety and experiment with various cooking techniques such as grilling, roasting or sautéing in order to bring variety in textures and flavors of dishes - the goal here should be making the plan enjoyable and sustainable part of life!
- **Tracking and Adjustment:** Once your 8-week meal plan begins, it's important to keep track of its progress

and adjust as necessary. Keep a list of recipes you enjoy most as you progress, modifications you made or new ingredient combinations you discovered that might come in handy later or create your own Mediterranean dishes beyond this short duration of eight weeks. This information can help customize future plans or help create Mediterranean inspired dishes beyond its lifespan!

Remember, an 8-week meal plan should serve as a guide on your journey towards leading a healthier lifestyle; but it shouldn't be seen as set in stone. Customization and adaptation is key in order to meet individual tastes, preferences, and dietary requirements; take this opportunity to discover Mediterranean flavors while trying new ingredients to craft something truly personalized for you! Savor every moment spent feeding yourself nutritious yet satiating dishes available through Mediterranean diet!

At its heart, successfully following an 8-Week No-Stress Meal Plan requires some advance preparation and customization. By employing meal prepping techniques and adapting it to suit your preferences, embracing Mediterranean way of eating becomes enjoyable experience. Remember, the ultimate aim being to nourish and discover new flavors while creating sustainable healthy eating practices with enjoyment! So take this exciting adventure headfirst; and let Mediterranean flavors inspire culinary creativity as well as overall well being!

CONCLUSION

As we come to the conclusion of The Mediterranean Cookbook for Beginners, it's time to reflect upon our culinary adventure and appreciate what knowledge and flavors we have gleaned along the way. In this book, we have explored Mediterranean cuisine's depths; discovering its secrets as well as health benefits it provides. From vibrant salads and appetizers to hearty soups and stews; delectable seafood dishes to decadent desserts; we have covered a vast variety of recipes which encapsulate its essence.

By exploring the Mediterranean diet, we have gained an appreciation of its core principles and components. We've become acquainted with its abundance of fresh fruits and vegetables, whole grains, lean proteins and healthy fats which form its foundation. Beyond providing sustenance for body and soul alike, Mediterranean cuisine offers celebration of flavor simplicity as well as sharing meals with loved ones.

At every turn in this journey, we have highlighted the numerous health advantages associated with the Mediterranean diet. Its emphasis on whole, unprocessed foods rich in nutrients and antioxidants has been scientifically shown to lead to positive health results; from reducing chronic disease risk reduction and heart health promotion to mental wellbeing support. Overall vitality and longevity have all seen great improvements from adhering to such a plan.

As you close this book, I encourage you to begin an ongoing relationship with Mediterranean cuisine. Experiment with the recipes you have learned and let your creativity flourish in the kitchen; adapt dishes according to your own taste, include seasonal produce whenever possible and invite your loved ones on your culinary adventure! Attaining a Mediterranean lifestyle doesn't involve temporary fixes or restrictive diet plans; rather, it should be seen as an enjoyable lifestyle change that lasts. Savoring vibrant ingredients while dining mindfully creates deeper connections between what we eat and those with whom we share it. Feeding our bodies' healthy meals while delighting our souls by cooking up delectable culinary creations is something everyone should experience at least once!

As you embrace the Mediterranean diet, remember that it is not an inflexible set of rules but instead provides a flexible framework that allows for personalization and adaptation. Let it inspire you to discover new flavors, ingredients, and dishes - and let it lead you on a journey towards healthier living while celebrating its joy!

The Mediterranean Cookbook for Beginners has provided you with access to an abundance of vibrant flavors, healthful ingredients and the art of Mediterranean cooking. I hope that this book has ignited your passion for Mediterranean cuisine and encouraged you to continue exploring its endless potential - may its flavors nourish your body while lifting your spirit - may they continue bringing joyous dinner tables around the globe for years! I wish you every success with your culinary adventure - bon appétit!

Milton Keynes UK
Ingram Content Group UK Ltd.
UKHW030640020224
437154UK00011B/442

9 798223 876519